Ethics - The State - The Person

Ethics and Policies

Artur Victoria

Published by Edições Esgotadas, 2023.

ETHICS - THE STATE - THE PERSON

First edition. March 2, 2023.

ISBN: 979-8230164098

Written by Artur Victoria.

PRESENTATION By Professor Ives Gandra d.a Silva Martins Ph.D*

Professor Artur Victória, an eminent Portuguese thinker, asked me to write a few lines about his new book entitled "Ethics - The State - The Person;' in which, in light of his reflection on Ethics, in the various manifestations of man in society and how the State and Governments should act, it offers the reader an admirable study to be meditated upon by anyone on the conduct of people and power holders in the world today, through well-defined goals. In the first chapter, he raises the nucleus, which will guide his writing, strictly taking the Treaty of Westphalia to modernity, which ended the 3D-year War, but generated solid States and opened up the field for the Enlightenment, responsible for the greatest bloodbath of French history, through the prism of the French Revolution.

However, it allowed the path to national democracies in the 19th and 20th centuries to be unveiled, despite totalitarian outbreaks, on the sowing of the road of economic, cultural, and political globalization. In his writing, divided into seven parts (introduction, ethical behavior having the public interest as its object, the ethical origins of public administration and all its consequences and aspects, the legal issue in the face of a theory of values, the reform of the State as presupposing a new model of community coexistence, the ever-present dilemma of defense and National Security and the environmental challenge), the eminent master permeates all the historical, sociological, political, economic, philosophical, legal, anthropological variables that shape human existence in today based on its evolution, seeking to direct the ultimate purposes of the State and the Person towards a model of possible Ethical valuation, in a society whose growth in technological knowledge has not corresponded to an improvement in the condition of a considerable portion of its inhabitants.

This year I launched a booklet that deduced similar concerns, entitled "The Era of Challenges;' subtitled "Humanity and the dilemmas of its permanence:' Some of the problems he dealt with in this magnificent work, Professor Artur Victoria, I also did it with many convergences and few divergences but cantered on the main one to be objectified by humanity, that is, the Ethical behaviour in facing the avalanche of obstacles to its existence, among which the Covid 19 pandemic is not the only one. I have examined the Ethical issue and the Moral issue under the double focus ofits origin; that is, although its translation from Greek and Latin represents "customs;' considered a bonus (ethos and mos, moris), its deontic content is distinct. The more speculative than pragmatic Greeks - despite their monumental philosophical and artistic work never managed to form a stable empire, experiencing the political phenomenon of small city-states - always saw Ethics as a set of principles to be more meditated and debated in the social gatherings to be implemented, not even their gods being role models. The Romans, on the contrary, were more pragmatic than speculative - imitators of the Greeks innovated in everything by shaping their law as an instrument of conquest that supported a European, North African and Middle East domination for 2,100 years, that is, from 753 BC until AD 1453- ended up talking to their law, which until today influences world civil law and other related branches, the sense of Morality, from Ethics of values to be lived. Bastiat, in the 19th century, in his book" TheLaw," said that its function was not to do justice but not to allow injustice. This thought expresses the concern to cover the legal system of countries with a blanket in which PRESENTATION 11 the valuation Ethics would have to be the main objective of the legislator, although, in practice, it is not. As a naturalist with a Thomist background, which I am, I consider that there is a central nucleus of the legal order, which is of Natural Law in all legal orders, which transcend positive law, such as, for example, the Charter of Natural Law, which is the declaration of Human Rights, embodied in almost all modern Constitutions. In this way, there would not be a clash between Natural and Positive Law, as there are norms that the State can only recognize and the vast majority that it can create, which is why the clash only occurs in legal regimes that do not respect fundamental Human Rights. These brief considerations, I recognize this well-elaborated work. I make these brief considerations, to recognize, in the well-prepared book by Professor Artur Vitoria which, in the wide range of suggestions he makes about Ethics for the State and the Person, in modernity, opens up a fantastic field of reflection for jurists, philosophers, economists, environmentalists, technocrats, politicians and professionals, in general, is an excellent book, which deserves to be read by as many as are interested in the fate of humanity. Congratulations!

* Professor Emeritus at Mackenzie Universities, UNlp, UNIFIEO, UNIFMU, CIEE/O ESTADO DE São Paulo, Army Command and General Staff Schools - ECEME, War Superior – ESG and the Magistracy of the Federal Regional Court - 1st Region; Honorary Professor at the Universities Austral (Argentina), San Martin de Porres (Peru) and Vasili Goldis (Romania); Doctor Honoris Causa at the Universities of Craiova (Romania) and PUCs-Parana and RS, and Professor at the University of Minho (Portugal); President of the Superior Law Council of FECOMERCIO - SP; former President of the Academia Paulista de Letras-APL and the Instituto dos Advogados de Sao Paulo-IASP.

PREFACE By Admiral Antonio Silva Ribeiro Ph.D*

"Ethics -The State -The Person" is a work in which Dr. Artur Victoria surprises the public with his unique capacity for pragmatic analysis of the major issues facing humanity in a globalised world where there is a constant and rapid change in the complex challenges posed by persistent political, economic, social, environmental and security uncertainties. In this context, it becomes imperative to reflect on the paths to follow in the search for peace and sustainable progress on a global scale. This work is written with exceptional quality and remarkable scientific rigour. These factors, together with the high esteem, friendship and consideration I have for Dr. Artur Victoria, were more than enough reasons to prompt me to accept to preface his new book. Artur Victoria is, without a doubt, a relevant figure in our society; with an academic background of excellence and a vast professional experience. The functions performed within the scope of the legal profession, as well as the positions of organizational leadership and institutional coordination he has held, in national and international non-governmental institutions, associated with the constant research and scientific production developed throughout his life, credit him as an eminent thinker and a reference in ethical, geopolitical, governmental and security issues. In fact, his thinking and critical capacity are clearly evident in this book, which opens doors for reflection by all those interested in the most

pressing questions facing the future of humanity, from the philosophical, legal, economic, political, social and environmental fields. To give the reader the context of the problem it sets out to address, Arthur Victoria refers his narrative to the Treaty of Westphalia, as the moment that was at the origin of International Law and the balance of power between sovereign nations, as we know them today. If, on the one hand, this event opened the doors to the Enlightenment, to rapid scientific advance and to liberal democracies, on the other hand, it was the harbinger of the end of empires, which culminated with the First World War, and of the emergence of totalitarian regimes that, in a generalised way, characterised Europe at the beginning of the 20th century, leading to the most striking conflict in the history of humanity, the Second World War.

More than 70 years after the end of this conflict, which gave rise to the United Nations Organization and whose inspiring principles, in the words of one of the most prominent Portuguese thinkers of our time - Professor Adriano Moreira - are "One Single World" and "Earth, the common home of Mankind" the challenges to world governance and peace remain and are rapidly changing.

Despite the efforts made by the international community and the scientific and technological advances that recent years have brought us, we have not witnessed a proportional evolution in the quality of life of the world's populations across the board. These factors necessarily lead us to consider that the concepts defending equal rights and human dignity, which should be at the heart of all national and international policies, are not valid if they are nothing more than theories proclaimed only by activists, without concerted intervention and mobilization by States. In this context, and also taking into consideration the two most recent events that have transformed societies and their way of life, referring of course to the COVID-19 pandemic and the armed conflict that has been raging in Ukraine since 24 February 2022, I am pleased to highlight the relevance of the topic addressed and the importance and depth of the author's impartial and objective, through, throughout the text, which he divides into three fundamental parts

- the State, the individual, and the environment - presenting, as a connecting thread, the elements of ethics and morality, which he considers to be the basis for resolving the major issues of public interest, in an increasingly dynamic, complex and unstable world.

As Yuval Noah Harari states in his book 21 Lessons for the 21st Century: " A global world puts unprecedented pressure on our personal conduct and morality': It is in this line of thought that the author begins by addressing the central role of the State in making decisions about what to do in the light of the great challenges of the 21st century, quickly changing the widespread habit of not defining future goals and not planning the necessary policies to achieve them. Within this framework, Artur Victoria discusses the main functions and responsibilities of the State and the importance of ethics for the public interest, corporations, the legal system and democracies. He also addresses the need for State reform with a view to a new model of community coexistence, the paradigm of national defence and security, and information systems.

In the chapter dedicated to the Person, Artur Victoria invites the reader to reflect on the ethics and morals that should govern every member of a changing society. For this, he considers it necessary a deep meditation process, in an intellectual exercise of balance between the definition of the ambitions and goals of each one, in order to find an answer to the question "(...) how should I live my life? (...)': The answers found must necessarily be compatible with those which overlap them, this is, those of society and the organisations to which each one belongs. However, the author takes this exercise of reflection further, addressing the need for the establishment of ethical and moral codes by governmental and non-governmental organisations, as an integral part of society. The analysis of such a deep and complex theme would not be complete without an adequate approach to the biggest problem facing the sustainable survival of humanity in the medium and long term.

It is in this context that Artur Victoria reflects on the environment and on the problem of climate change resulting from mankind's exploitation of natural resources, associated with the exponential growth of the world's population since the beginning of the 19th century. The reader is also invited to meditate on the paradigm of behavioural change and environmental awareness, as well as on alternative strategies to be outlined for an economically and financially sustainable development, based on the maintenance of social and cultural values of the different populations, with scientific research and technological development playing an absolutely key role in the necessary advances towards an intelligent sustainability on a planetary scale.

He conclude with the conviction that, in a world that is increasingly uncertain and full of irrelevant information, and in which ethics is often forgotten by governments and organisations, causing

States and individuals to behave in deviant ways, reason gives us the power to better define the direction to follow in the search for a more prosperous, egalitarian, safe and sustainable future for humanity.

This book by Artur Victoria certainly contributes to that goal, providing the reader with a clear vision of the issues that must be analysed and reflected upon, in the certainty that the approach to ethics applied to the State and to the person is the key we need to foster the hope necessary for the perpetuation of our civilisation as we know it. As Professor Adriano Moreira said, it is imperative not to allow the "creed of interests" to override the "creed of value".

* Admiral Antonio Silva Ribeiro has been Chief of Staff of the Armed Forces since March 1,2018. Admiral Antonio Silva Ribeiro, together it's the military career, is also an academic specializing in the areas of Strategy; Political Science, and History. In his academic career, he is a visiting professor at the Instituto Superior de Ciências Socials e Politicas, with a specialization in Strategy. He is also a military teacher at the Naval School. He is the author of sixteen books, three of them with international editions. He has delivered over 130 lectures and has over 300 articles published in national and international newspapers and magazines.

THE STATE

The method involved assuming liberal vote-based qualities and standardizing them for a worldwide call to no end edification. A particularly worldwide enlightenment should intend to edify the inexorably merciless universe of financial matters; similarly, in the eighteenth century, Enlightenment started the method involved with socializing the absolutist post-Westphalia States.

It is inside this setting that it is contended that the decay of the State and the moving premise of political authenticity legitimize philanthropic 'intercession; especially to forestall the persecution of those whose permission has not been looked for by people with significant influence. But, without a doubt, as the dividers around Sovereign States separate the term 'mediation' that appears to be less and less suitable and loses quite a bit of its standardizing shame.

At first, the new States were profoundly dictators - a tyranny supported by the dread of inward disarray. The North Atlantic Enlightenment humanized such States in the eighteenth century and friendly liberals in the nineteenth century. Edification nonconformists demanded that States legitimize themselves by facilitating residents' privileges and becoming responsible to the population.

Responsibility components were refined through fair assemblies and regulatory Law. Social liberals looked to expand the scope of Rights the developing State for its residents. The individuals who didn't look for millenarian upset appeared to hold fast to a basically Whig hypothesis of history, of steady improvement towards a typical endpoint in which the Rights got by liberal vote-based social orders were extended, and the quantity of such social orders expanded. What all speculations accepted was the presence of a solid-State. The discussions were regarding what should be applied to its administration - freedom, equity, rights, citizenship, popular government, region, government assistance, and Law and Order.

Scopes of late patterns, which are prevalently labelled 'globalization: have shaken the presumption that a universe of solid Sovereign States was the normal condition to which humanity was developing. A long time since the Treaty of Westphalia can be found in diverse light on a fundamental level. Maybe then a cycle in which specific geographic regions were politically solidified as States, this period could now be deciphered as a somewhat short intermission to improve political networks and political establishments.

Sovereign States are not the endpoint of an established turn of events but rather a simple momentary stage. The political and financial powers have subverted the presumption of the solid-State as the setting for political discussion about the adjusting and acknowledging of liberal majority rule esteems.

The two doubters and allies of globalization have questioned the significance of State-based hypotheses and qualities. These qualities were framed in and for solid States. Citizenship, majority rule Government assistance, and the local area reference sovereign States but need obvious application in a bigger, more diffuse worldwide world The establishments which advance support and understand those qualities are a lot of State-based The rights, obligations, and feeling of having a place that goes with citizenship are connected to State establishments. The majority rule Government is acknowledged through resident support in the councils of States and their administrative components. However, it has less mileage if the genuine force and scope of decision open to those lawmaking bodies is restricted.

1. Ethical Behaviour is a Solution for the Public Interest

Try to change institutions to emphasize and reinforce Ethical behaviour, promote rather than discourage those who would be ethical, and make unethical behaviour more difficult to perform and easier to detect.

The issues and answers must be found in the blend of Law, Morals, and Institutional plans. These incredible threesomes of elements which all things considered, shape how our establishments perform structure what David Wood called my "set of three." Specialists were never delighted with this term and have messed with "triangle," and "carriage:'

In any case, it currently appears that the most applicable term, if disrespect can be renounced, is "trinity" - a bunch of components that can be seen independently but sum to various parts of an entirety. The defence of public area organizations is to serve some expressed local area worth. Simultaneously, those organizations would be kept from doing so to benefit from different qualities like Common Liberties. These roads might be shut down off by criminal or common assents, by guideline, by authoritative Law, by Parliamentary investigation (or examination by some exceptionally established body like an Ombudsman), by Councils, by exposing public area associations to standard endorsement necessities, obligations to give ecological or administrative effect articulations.

Time and again, regulatory Law falls into the snare of attempting to guarantee that administrative force isn't utilized such that it does accidental mischief instead of endeavouring to guarantee that it is practiced to additional the worth which supported the force in any case. By such combinations of measures, the Law should be used to push institutions into fulfilling the purposes that justify them.

1.1. Ethical origins of Public Administration

The Ethics will be seen as partly self-generated (though self-interpreted) rather than handed down from on high - in drafting specific codes. However, it is one thing for general implicit rules to require community workers to "try to accomplish the best expectations practicable." There are many motivations behind Laws, and expressing clear standards and authorizing breaks are just two among many. We feature somewhere around three sorts of such Laws. The first is the place where forcing an authorization (even a positive assent or prize) isn't the point. One of the favourites is Tony Honore's example of the rule "the age of majority is 18": The second is found in the move towards "fuzzy law." There is a developing appreciation that it is unrealistic to determine rules to cover each circumstance. Instead, enactment should focus on articulating the core values instead of doing something absurd and covering each possibility.

This takes to obvious result - where the justification endorsement demonstrates the significance of the standard instead of the connected approval. The ideas of sway and intercession are firmly interwoven. The jurisdictional dividers raised along the limits of country express make the obstructions to 'global mediation. If less importance were put on those limits, the legitimate and political ideas of "worldwide mediation" would lose their importance, and various ideas would be required. Sway is under challenge on two fronts:

1) The first is how the powers of globalization are debilitating the uprightness and strength of Sovereign States. They are essentially changing the institutional setting of' solid States depends on autonomous political networks, which has given the presumptions on which established and global Law have been based.

2) The second lies in a principal shifting the premise of political authenticity from adequacy (or the earlier effective utilization of power) to the dynamic permission of the represented. These difficulties will have significant ramifications for how we ponder States, residents, and the communications between them. Those results will incorporate contentions about Power and intercession, the essential subject of this part. Yet, they will stretch out a long way past that to the whole philosophical setting inside which such discussions are led. The powers of globalization give a critical test to liberal popularity-based qualities - including freedom, rights, majority rules system, equity, citizenship, local area, government assistance, and Law and Order.

1.2. Ethical Justification on the Public Administration

The defence of a public area establishment can give the premise to the morals of its overseers. This can assist with demonstrating what people should avoid doing subsequently. The main task of Morals is disclosing to us how we should carry on with our lives or, in public areas Morals, how we should act inside our authoritative jobs. Moreover, the support of an establishment highlights the foundation and movement inside it. It can recommend the objectives individuals should set themselves and practice their forces under that participation.

It sets out the positive accomplishments that an executive should decide by her companions and pass judgment on herself. Morals continually bring up the issue of what structure, plan, and connections among individuals and representatives of an institution will probably help accomplish the qualities that legitimize having a public area organization.

Additionally brings up the adverse issue of how we can prevent a portion of the deviations that forestall it accomplishing those qualities. Be that as it may, likewise with Law and Morals, the essential accentuation is on what they can decidedly accomplish. Thus, we should ask what sort of institutional structure is more likely to allow public sector agencies to fulfil their established values. Such a justification should provide a reason for blocking off expenses by which money provided for such purposes is expended for other ends and removing incentives for them to do so. At the same time, those institutions would be prevented from doing so at the expense of different values such as Human Rights.

1.3. Ethics in public services

Open body supervisors are entrusted to convey administrations to people in general. Subsequently, it would help guarantee that the administrations you give are compelling, proficient, and dependable Yet, their conveyance is liberated from debasement and misbehaviour. Furthermore, individuals should get a reasonable comprehension of the significant elements of public bodies and the commitments of your institution and yourselves as specified in the Law. Essential aspects of public bodies are booked by Law as loose bodies.

They are assigned because their tasks and administrations significantly affect the general population's interests and society overall. For example, they are the:

- Major services providers given a monopoly/ franchise/license by the Government like bus companies, railway companies;
- Organizations spending/disbursing substantial public funds, e.g., universities, hospitals;
- Organizations performing public regulatory functions, e.g., regulatory bodies of the financial sector and real estate industry;
- Organizations performing other essential public service functions, e.g., housing and land development bodies, charitable organizations; and
- Major mass media organizations, e.g., television and broadcasting stations.

1.4. Public management is a public trust

Open body leaders should guarantee that their activities are led reasonably and dependably.

Your staff keeps a high unmistakable norm of lead, so honest trust is maintained and public interest secured. Morals and qualities ought to be educated in policy implementation schools. Moral standards can be educated. However, they can't be equally instructed because persons show different abilities and information on planning, data innovation, workforce, board, strategy investigation, and so forth.

The second extraordinary conflict of the twentieth century brought legislative issues/organization division to its knees. Executives are and ought to be enthusiastic fewer gadgets of general labour and products, in this manner opening up restoration of policy management. New Public Service was promoted by Denhardt and Denhardt (2000). His vision is that government leader's return to their foundations as "guardians of democracy": In addition, formulate rules that, independently and collectively, provide a standardization framework for the seasoned government administrator. However, recovery will not be an easy task for the experienced.

Affiliates, policymakers, or people who work daily make their networks the ideal place to live, work and play. A little help can be found in the variety of exhibits and recently distributed items. Reopen and reload. As the conversation progresses, you are undoubtedly aging within the base. Adams and Balfour'scall to expose regulatory evil did not go unnoticed. Must do, can do, and should be commended. As it is often expressed but only occasionally heard, public assistance is a noble calling. Perhaps we should help ourselves remember this every day and use this inclination to intensify our work as teachers and government officials. The result is likely to be a significant rediscovery and restoration of policy implementation as an area of research and practice.

1.5. Setting the Powers of Public Servants

Laws should explain what community workers can do and why they have been given those forces. Officials ought to conscientiously consider why force is given and guarantee that they provide just the required forces. (This ought to be differentiated by the propensity to offer extensive powers to public authorities.

It isn't shocking where Laws are as often as possible proposed by similar community workers who practice them). This makes legal audit and regulatory Law, by and large, simpler because no one can decipher ambiguities in the powers given as far as the reasons for which they are given and the avocations for doing as such (Kelly, 2021). 1.1 The Ethical Relationship in the Corporate and Public Sector There are several reasons why some are reluctant to apply business Ethics to public sector Ethics.

2.1. Public/Private Distinction

People who are firmly rated between "public" and "private" may also seek to acknowledge the Morality of their agents. Be that as it may, the ratings are periodically reviewed. The similarities between significant Government institutions and large non-administered entities are, in most cases, more informative than their differences. In particular, we saw strong similarities in the types of support for public and private companies.

Public authorities can use force and are held to higher legal standards. They are considered sound superior principles for the most part. However, the power of various authorities to influence residents equates to the power of large companies. While there are many differences in value and degree, it can be argued that the strength of each significant institution (Government, organization, and institution) creates a moral obligation.

Institutional strength is a state of comparability, not a difference between corporate and Government Morality. Consequently, the vast majority of sources of conflict between business and Government as a whole will be exaggerated or of minor importance compared to Morality which must be explored in the same way.

Suddenly, the Morality of Government and business raises comparative questions, similar questions, and demands comparable measures. The problems of business and Government that lead to cries of "morality" are, in fact, problems at the heart of the essential foundations of society. Very few governmental or commercial institutions do not satisfy the abuse that legitimizes the Power and advantage that are accumulated in their hands.

These funds must support agreements and use these resources to develop appropriate legal principles, moral guidelines, and institutional structures. It does not mean that the problems or agreements are indistinguishable; organizations differ in their defences and institutional structures that lose or maintain their recognition.

The difference lies in the idea of these legitimating and the institutional structures that can understand them, not in whether they are currently in the hands of the Government and not of the companies. It is common knowledge that we cannot operate based on the guiding principles of the Public Sphere authorities based on Morality alone.

Morality is part of the cycle through which improvement can be achieved. Still, ultimately it must include legal change and an institutional model. Interaction consists of examining the establishment's defences, from which the three components of the trinity (David Wood) can be identified.

The attempt to institutionalize public sector Ethics is co-occurring as the State is updating its administrative Law and reforming the organization of its public service.

2.2. Ethical Risk Mitigation

People who have worked longer to eliminate hazards say they perceive the work as a systematic and mental demand in ways they couldn't wait for. Meanwhile, others do not see the need for something new to ensure control of hazards. Work, where it is genuinely critical, must be assigned through the existing line structures - executive structures. Every utility leader is aware of the dangers in their regions and copes with them.

This methodology separates in the most punctual stage when managers request the identification of hazards or weak points to consider. When the job of controlling hazards will only be assigned in the future, administrators will generally distinguish only those hazards they are aware of Organizations manage hazards that are undetectable or uncertain.

Underrepresented risks or not in typical cyclical flows, abnormal sizes, and dimensions (hence, without falling directly into the scope of responsibility (division) or shared (where collaboration with different offices is a precondition for a decisive intervention) International and global hazards have a more significant scale or hazard level greater than available control systems.

The accurate models are rising temperatures across the Earth, the emergence of insurmountable diseases, massacres, and global psychological oppression. Bullying is limited by the absence of any focal control system or any legitimate command or position to follow up on a sufficiently broad front.

Inevitably knowledgeable opponents are involved; the business of "control" is becoming a unique and never-ending game against intruders who seek to circumvent control activities. Examples of such adversaries include fear mongers, drug dealers, extortionists and criminals. Their greatness is often insecure, generating a genuine interest in leadership.

Control systems must constantly take into account hostile transformations. Mastering a control match requires scrutiny of the opponents' actions and understanding and undermining their methodologies.

Control of hazards becomes a round of understanding and counter cognition, like sexual or actual abuse. The orderly evaluation is crucial to promote a viable control activity. Proactive, in-house work is needed to verify and locate, help uncover the true nature and extent of the hazard, and ensure that mediation is planned around the natural risk.

The dangers in which anticipation is primarily anticipated involve unthinkable setbacks, for example, atomic or organic psychological warfare. Assessing the probability and size of a hazard is incredibly difficult. It becomes difficult to control the financial plan. The standard does not joke with a flaw. Given the absence of apparent disasters, it is inherently dangerous to legitimize the costs of such work.

Similarly, it is challenging to quantify preventive application. When risk-taking performance is enhanced, lifestyles can reward and even celebrate the undue danger taken by people who can get and "deal with it:' On the other hand, coercion to execute can force workers to "push themselves to the limit; which is very close to tragedy.

2.3. Ethical Risk Control

Institutions' needs, operations, and lifestyles can make it difficult to cope with hazards. Hazard control activities can conflict with the "important and influential" means practiced in the event of suspected fiduciary management. Claims should be planned and their viability evaluated (to the extent possible) in the chain of potential cases.

All work must be considered to control, coordinate, and be directed backward to eliminate hazards. Research is often essential to segregate hazards, preventing or reducing predecessors. Institutions may want to deprive people who have fallen over the edge rather than abandon presentation earnings. Discipline after a fall may result in a demonstration, as the institution will hesitate to give-up the exhibition benefit. The institution may be reluctant to return assets for inspection, observation, and approval.

At a minimum, a risk-management system must have the following components:

• A nomination system that generates and routes nominations for risks that need to be addressed.

• Personnel resource allocation system for risk mitigation projects.

• Project records: project files, paper or electronic, organized around risks or concentrations of risks (rather than around cases, programs, systems, or functional units).

Agencies are learning to organize resources around essential risk areas respecting the natural shape and size of the problems. They seek to solve, rather than imposing them on existing organizational structures.

As they reflect on their hard-won successes, agency leaders typically find that the following observations apply to their successful risk control initiatives.

• Neither specific risk components nor a solution has been provided for anywhere in the agency legislation. Therefore, solving the problem of mitigating the risk did not require a change in legislation or general agency policies.

• The "problem" or "concentration of risk" has been identified, resolved, and resolved below the level of strategic planning. While broad risks may be identified in an agency's mission statement, authorizing legislation, and strategic plans, successful projects are usually carefully outlined.

• Risk performance indicators (indicators of success in risk mitigation) were project-specific and were selected before developing the action plan. Therefore, developing appropriate metrics required as much creativity and imagination as the action plan itself. Real-world problems come in awkward shapes and sizes that don't fit well-established groups or units. Dealing with them requires coordination and commitment from different departments and agencies.

• Management does not understand this kind of work and does not support those who try it.

• Problem-solving and risk mitigation work bring an unfamiliar degree of discretion and an uncertain degree of authorization. Innovative agencies find this work unusual, unrelentingly challenging, and demanding intellectual effort. Many government agencies, primarily regulatory and law enforcement agencies, are implementing a risk management system to reorient their core business.

Many others recognize the need to use formal risk management approaches to protect their people, customers, resources, and ability to perform their core tasks.

2.4. Ethical Conflict

The actual excuse to cut the case in moderation is that you need a fight. Disagreement is the essence of a decent case conversation: it draws people in; it makes them think carefully and defend their position; and this shows them that while there are no generally correct answers, there are solid questions.

Most cases are controversial: a social approach that people disagree on; administrative elections involving unpleasant compromises; a morally schematic political device.

An essential task of specialist training is to give students practice solving complex scientific and managerial problems. Cases that raise earnest questions are an ideal guided practice. Regardless, the fight can be subtle. Like a hallucination, something that resembles a situation at a distance cannot be a phenomenon at a closer distance. For example, a director does not have many activity options, considering the political realities that assume the evaluative standards are strongly inclined towards choosing an approach. In that case, there is no room for controversy and, therefore, for the discussion of the case.

Controversial issues were not evident in a quick analysis of the case. Distinguishing them required a deep understanding of the situation on the part of the teacher and a deep understanding of what the trendsetters probably didn't take into account. Disagreements, even about examples of how to cope with adversity, tend to focus on the choice.

Teachers keep track of the fact that everything else is equal. The case works best if you leave this choice unresolved, that is, if it represents a decision or choice that goes against the principal or examiner without revealing what the hero did and the results of this activity.

The case of allowing doubles to make decisions demonstrates a more viable way of making them accept an essential individual point of view rather than looking from an external point of view. Moreover, the requirement of a substantial choice gives a sense of speed to the circumstances. Whatever the configuration, the decisive choice is critical for the future case.

People can reflectively evaluate the vast underlying authority procedure. It will be more helpful for them to choose a seemingly small problem that solves the biggest critical issue facing the leader in the microcosm. In any case, when problems with education are clarified in advance, this is not a guarantee. The case can end in something very unique (paper records are in some places similar to the notes provided by long-term individual meetings). Furthermore, the case regularly ends with many more questions than expected. However, the earlier it is possible to determine the probable demonstrative capacity, the more skilful and viable it will be.

3. Ethics on the Judiciary

• Listen to magistrates and officials about concerns and doubts in applying the Code of Judicial Ethics.

• Guide and Advise on the interpretation and application of Ethical regulations through advisory opinions.

• Receive, diligence, and register complaints and Ethical consultations, in addition to investigating the alleged facts.

• Promote special recognitions in favour of judges and officials who have dignified judicial work.

• Develop action programs that promote compliance with the Code of Judicial Ethics The sole purpose of the Code of Judicial Ethics is to achieve excellence in the justice service, positively impacting all social sectors, including the justice operators themselves. The faithful and complete fulfilment of the justice demands in judging body the concurrence of a series of qualities and virtues that make in the profile of the magistrates not only intellectual values but also Ethical Values. The legal element cannot be isolated from the moral component. Likewise, the Judge cannot be conceived outside or independently of Moral Rules destined to regulate his functional and personal conduct. There can be no Law without justice or justice without Ethics.

Why is it essential to comply with the Code of Ethics? Society legitimated the Magistrates and judicial officials to exercise the jurisdictional function. They must warranty the Fundamental Right of the population to have access to independent, impartial, transparent, responsible, efficient, effective, and equitable justice. Judicial Ethics acts as a regulatory guideline for this exercise.

3.1. Justifications and Principle of Ethics and Law

Each new law, new institutional change, and new area-wide arrangement ought to be shipped off the Morals office for guidance on whether it represents any Moral danger and on the off chance that it very well may be shifted such that supports increasing expectations or lessening debasement.

Numerous new strategy recommendations are systems as opposed to forcing their thoughts of morals on the organization. Morals are one region that just can't be forced from the interaction should survey authoritative law standards in the light of the moral codes taken on.

The objective ought not to be to imitate the Code of Morals in managerial Law; however, to pose a comparative inquiry to that is asked concerning criminal punishments: when should an inability to keep moral guidelines lead to lawful results - for this situation, the nullification of choice? The unfortunate results for the workplace are far less, and the positive outcomes are critical.

As they and their partners have looked into the detail of their forces and obligations and have been helped to remember why they hold those Powers, authoritative Law need just be used at a lot higher point on the standardizing continuum (Kelly, 2021).

We ought not to get snatched up by Regulatory Law as a method for 'upholding' morals because this missteps the connection between morals and law. Morals should, in any case, work all the more straightforwardly through the cognizant comprehension of public authorities and by taking earlier exhortation where they are in question. In any case, the blend of moral standard-setting and authoritative law ought to be investigated further and taken advantage of without limit. All laws should be deciphered, and ambiguities and vulnerabilities are unavoidable. There are two different ways of managing this.

- The first is to attempt to determine everything about it.
- The second is to stress the motivations behind endorsement and the standards fundamental it as a manual for translation by the people who are relied upon to follow it and the appointed authorities who might be approached to settle it. Current practice is progressively underlining the last-mentioned while never shunning the previous. The proposed look for legitimizations of public foundations esteems that can illuminate the laws that administer those organizations. Such qualities furnish the way to synchronize them with moral standard-setting and institutional change.

The standards hidden new and existing endorsement ought to be plainly expressed and the text of the enactment considered guaranteeing that it is reliable with those standards. Nobody ought to be more able to decide the standards fundamental to the enactment than the individuals who draft it, and nobody ought to be fit for making the law reliable and intelligible around those standards (Kelly, 2021).

Regardless, nobody ought to make law except if they comprehend and set out the reasons it is expected to accomplish and the standards it ought to further. Those standards ought to be the primary thing on the plan of the drafters and for the lawmakers who pass it into law.

Luckily, lawmakers are more capable of considering standard than detail given their bustling timetables, their restricted abilities to focus, and (suitably) fluctuated foundations. A decent idea is that councils should consider themselves to be, as a matter of first importance, a 'discussion of standard: Laws sanctioned by the Fundamental Assembly ought to contain the standards, the fundamental arrangements, the forces given to authorities, offenses and punishments for the break, the fixing of assessments and charges, and the protections for residents.

More point-by-point arrangements can be passed on to subordinate endorsement, which can be refreshed (however still dependent upon dismissal by either assembly chamber). Where the Assembly (or, more probable, its Scrutiny of Legislation Committee) needs to see how the principle performance and subordinate enactment connect, it might require the proposed subordinate ratification to be postponed all the while as the real one enactment (Kelly, 2021). The other option in contrast to giving subtleties is through the courts, which decipher the enactment on account of debates. It will, by and large, be less alluring, proficient, and limitlessly more costly than setting out subtleties in subordinate enactment.

3.2. Ethical Value of the Law

The court's power- neither overwhelmed by cash nor sword- !ays essentially on open trust in its Ethical authorizations. Felix Frankfurter It is a fundamental barrier in convincing authorities and residents to stay away from degenerated conduct. It builds up Moral Guidelines and gives some conceivably solid motivations to those not (even though the apparent probability of discovery restricts the strength of those reasons). Notwithstanding, the principal game is somewhere else. Law plays a part to play in that 'fundamental game' by making institutional designs, setting out the forces of public authorities, and checking the activity of those forces under legal survey (Kelly, 2021). There are multiple methods of moving past best practices. The greater part of them guarantees that the Law is 'in synchronize' with Moral Principles and Institutional change.

The three work as a 'trinity' instead of as divergent, awkward, and conceivably clashing honesty measures. Law can assume various parts - demonstrating satisfactory and inadmissible conduct is, giving motivations to activity, eliminating wrongdoers from the position where they can re-affront, making organizations and constructions, giving survey instruments, and so forth.

Each law that has a section to play in the respectability arrangement of locale ought to be considered as far as the job it is expected to play and the job that it can play and be revised likewise. In this interaction, drafters and lawmakers ought to consistently know that laws are more useful than just monumental higher punishments. They ought to likewise know about the worth of laws that pronounce values and the resources to accomplish those qualities (Kelly, 2021).

Nonetheless, where punishments are involved, thought ought to be given to the mischief brought about by debasement and the types of punishment that will weigh most intensely with likely guilty parties.

3.3. The Laws Reflect and Back up Ethical Codes

Following the overall population area Moral Code's drawing up the laws making offenses for public authorities and the individuals who manage them ought to be rethought to guarantee that they play their fence job.

Public area reformers ought to think about what legitimate assents ought to be forced on the regulating continuum. Furthermore, laws ought to be re-drafted in phrasing that mirrors the moral standards they are supporting. Such laws ought to be considered for their consistency with Moral Principles, guaranteeing that the most shocking moral breaks are condemned and that moral conduct isn't.

3.4. The Judiciary - Some Aspects of Vulnerability

Regarding the confirmation of the judiciary, the judicial model is the principle of the balance, according to which the distribution of powers between National Power and the State was essentially fixed and immutable.

Enforcing International Law When activities involve using Power against others, it shouldn't do not simply deny those. It strikes against under the Law but also deny the security of that law. Powerless bandits endure exile and discipline. Tough runaways will generally turn into despots. The moment a neighbour's police officer uses a power that exceeds the law, the harassment becomes significant. The moment a security officer hands over the helicopter and stores the combat missiles, it is, frankly, intimidating. At best, this is the kind of security that Hobbes promoted. However, the best is sometimes realistic due to the humiliating impact of such a force, and the West has betrayed such systems since the time of Locke and embraced the Enlightenment. Law and Order are some of the most critical aspects of the North Atlantic Enlightenment.

The Rule of Law and order has become more entrenched and has received more visible formulation and institutional support than anywhere else. Of the many positive aspects of the Enlightenment, it is the one that requires the least orderly work to be applied in the world. It should simply apply outside of the solid Sovereign States for which it was initially conceived. There is a lack of confidence in global institutions to implement this law, and perhaps the associated pomp that local institutions can act as such. Law and order cannot be divided and limited within the boundaries of the Enlightenment States.

It must go global and organize itself into genuinely global organizations. Arguing that global standards should replace

Government authority also means recognizing that similar global standards override your actions in favour of Government Authority. Arguably, it worked out in the end.

Be that as it may, the question is who is the closure for? You can never overcome Sovereign limitations with conversations at board. If the initial shell in which is the guarantee that conversation is all-encompassing, then at this point, there can be nothing wrong with giving the decision to the body that has gone beyond its limits, which is inspired by it as much as possible.

Everyone knows a well-known fact. Otherwise, it shows that this is not all or that issues of personal public responsibility cloud his judgment. States try to hold another State and the people who run them accountable for their actions. However insisting on lowering the barriers around other States requires accepting the lowering of the barriers around the States seeking to justify intervention, at least for that intervention (and for the matters for which intervention is sought).

In seeking to make the subject State accountable to the International Community and its norms, or the National Community and its norms, intervening states must be accountable for their actions.

4. Democracy

Democracy is a political regime that has generated extensive literature, strongly polysemic in its reflection but raising relevant questions within debate. Democracy aims at the construction of a social ideal under democratic canons that then serve as minimum requirements for its adoption. When we discuss democracy, there are some degree of confusion due to the simple fact that democracy refers to both an ideal and reality. Continuing with the same, Schumpeter pointed out that democratic theory was simply a method, affirming that democracy is a neutral theory that is not associated with any particular ideal or end (Hanson, 2015).

However, there would not be any fully democratized regime for which a concept must be constructed: polyarchy (the government of multiple minorities). Polyarchies meet - to a greater or lesser degree - two fundamental requirements: opposition (or public debate) and participation. These characteristics imply having a voice in a public debate system, which would translate into greater opposition and participation, a better evaluation of democracy. It follows from this idea that democracy would be the competition of local elites to achieve power, at which time citizens can choose from a wide range of candidates (Hanson, 2015).

The harmony that is achieved with any of them will depend on whether the ideas contained in a given program interpret a particular feeling. Therefore, his analysis would have a close relationship between the electorate and the act of consuming, where the democratic element would be defined or determined by electoral competition.

4.1. National Integration

Democracy, Integration, and Development are terms that, as much as they are directly related, represent progress for a country. Communitarian and integration are related, attending to the concepts of Sovereignty and supranational order. Thus it is pointed out that regional integration is not incompatible with National Sovereignty, on the contrary, integration increases qualitatively the Sovereignty of the Member States, and regarding the supranational order, integration generates a legal community, a common law, typical of the member States and supranational organizations concerning these (Hanson,2015).

Economic integration constitutes a political strategy since it is an instrument that, taken advantage of for the benefit of the member countries, could make it possible to achieve the objective of political and economic reaffirmation in a world of growing inequality and unbridled ambitions of penetration and of power.

The free trade zone or free transit is one of the modes of organization of community action, and it consists of the formation of a space shaped by the territory of the member countries, within which obstacles of any nature (tax, technical, bureaucratic, etc.) that oppose, impede or hinder the free movement of goods or services.

Given above, several questions arise that will be addressed in the development of this work. Latin America is an important geographical area of the world, which constantly struggles to achieve and maintain political stability and thus contributes to its economic and social development. A relevant manifestation of globalization is the interest of the countries in trade liberalization, and in this sense, the treaties on the matter should ensure better living conditions for the inhabitants of the countries involved, which translates into progress and development (Hanson, 2015).

In Latin America, there is an experience on the implementation of free trade agreements, and the effects have been diverse, although the advantages are not always wide. Integration must contribute to the development of Nations and the strengthening of their democratic system, and to this extent, it is intended to guarantee improvements in the quality of life of the people.

4.2. Sovereignty

Intervention on the internal affairs of States has historically existed with different manifestations (military, economic, political, as well as direct or covert). Since the Peace of Westphalia and the rise of the Nation-State, it has been recognized that such acts should not be allowed. The idea of formulating non-intervention as a rule of conduct in relations between states began to take shape in the seventeenth century. With the frequent interference of the United States in Latin America came the initiative to establish non-intervention as a legal norm. Its initial formulation took place in American international law and was later incorporated into the UN and OAS Letters. But the criterion that any international action in internal affairs was inadmissible began to change in the 1970s when Human Rights were recognized as a legitimate matter of international concern, and their protection and validity ceased to be something exclusive to domestic jurisdiction. That produced a reinterpretation of non-intervention and its scope.

Based on this criterion, a process of expanding international involvement to the sphere of representative democracy later began which has also had its normative development and is part of contemporary international law. As a result, multilateral action in internal affairs has been expanding, and this has further reduced the field of non-intervention (Paphiti, 2011).

In recent decades, new spaces for international cooperation have been opened with State institutions, and external support has been extended to those related to the administration of justice. This reflects the evolution of the scope and interpretation of non-intervention.

Globalization has brought about various transformations in the concept of Sovereignty as the State has been affected in its limits and control inside and outside, although without a doubt, its role in international relations remains irreplaceable.

Sovereignty is limited insofar as it imposes barriers to the actions of other States that seek to attempt, intervene or fail to recognize commitments endorsed by international law, without entering into these actions the protection of Human Rights and the Environment. In this sense, and also taking up the principle of self-determination and that of non-intervention, there is a problem as more and more humanitarian, actions cover up acts of interference. This is why it is imperative to prosecute humanitarian assistance and/or interference (Paphiti, 2011).

As Corwin points out, the people are the highest source from which authority and order come, as they are the highest incarnation of the human will. The idea of Sovereignty can be identified in the Roman world. From the ancient times of the monarchy, it was understood that the ultimate political authority rested with the people and that, therefore, the king's Imperium originated in a special law approved by the assembly of curiae for such purposes. Later, both in the Digest and in the Institutions, it will be stated that what pleases the prince has the force of law since the people have granted him their power and authority. Thus, although the lex Regia handed over legislative powers to the emperor, in Roman culture, a fiction was maintained in which the people not only continued to be the source of legislation but also the people who legalized and legitimized the powers exercised. Therefore, the idea of a foundational authority of the Roman people was of common acceptance since the Law came from the will and was also nourished by the customs of the citizens (Paphiti, 2011).

The emergence of the theory of Parliamentary Sovereignty occurs from the disputes between the Crown and Parliament, which occurred in the seventeenth century, and in which the latter emerged as the winner. The arbitrariness and dangerousness characteristic of the absolute power exercised by the monarch did not vitiate Parliament. On the contrary, the proportional and egalitarian composition of the latter meant that his exercise of Absolute Power was not feared, while any kind of restriction on it was unnecessary.

With the "Glorious Revolution", the theory was consolidated, and the British Parliament assumed absolute sovereignty as an organ from which the laws emanated and to which it was not subject, thus being superior to all power and right within the State.

4.3. Political Parties

Funding Recent History

The financial resources of politics are fewer subjects of questions than the expenses of candidates and political organizations. Are they not, for example, credited with effects on the outcome of electoral competitions and sources of political inequalities? However, some resources have come to be the subject of extensive investigation because of their controversial nature. The challenge of is dual: To present some work by foreign researchers representative of the major themes constituting these research sectors and give the reader some comparative empirical benchmarks. The first scientific work on political financing emerged in the late 1920sand early 1930sin the United States. Three political scientists took hold of the subject and made it a legitimate academic subject. James K. Pollock was the first of these with Party Campaign Funds and Money, which is the first work to neglect the United States and deliberately move towards studying the financing of elections and political organizations in Great Britain, Germany, and France.

A long-time figurehead in political history, political parties are poor today since they arouse an increasingly limited interest. This observation, however, should not lead to pessimism. Because if classical type research is marking time, new fields and new questions are emerging - which are spurred in particular by sociology and political science. It's wise to:

- To study the political culture of a party as a factor of inertia,
- To identify the often conflicting stratifications of the militant generations;
- To relate the sociological composition of members to the definition and evolution of the party program,
- To appreciate the organization's weight in the life of the party;
- To observe the power games within the leadership.

So many stimulating issues are explaining, according to him, (James K. Pollock) the renewed interest in this type of historical research. How has the renewal of the partial history built around questions, methods, sources, and relays in France.

The history of parties benefits from other neighbourhoods, such as dynamic cultural history. Important work on militant propaganda and its evolution linked to the modernization of the media has revealed new issues. The legislator adopted numerous provisions relating to financing political life and electoral campaigns, intended to ensure their transparency.

Political parties receive State aid, which is now their main funding source and depends on their election results. In return, donations from other legal entities should be prohibited. Candidates for election must respect a spending limit set by law and may also receive public assistance. To benefit from it, they must track all of their expenses and income in a campaign account, which is the responsibility of a financial representative they appoint and who is presented by a chartered accountant.

The political parties and the candidates for the elections must face numerous expenses, the financing of which was, in most countries, framed by no precise legal regime. This gap had favoured certain abuses, which have been put an end to by successive keys since that date. Like any association, parties can collect contributions from their members. These contributions from members often represent only a very small part of the party's resources (the contribution collected from local elected representatives and member parliamentarians is generally higher). However, the practice varies greatly from one party to another.

Each year, funds intended to be paid to political parties and groups are entered into the finance law. In addition to the financing of political parties and electoral campaigns, one of the legislator's objectives was to ensure the transparency of the assets of elected officials, to prevent them from being able to take advantage of their elective functions to enrich themselves unduly. The obligation to declare assets has been instituted and filed at the start and end of the mandate.

Since the entry into force of organic Law relating to the transparency of Public Life, this reporting obligation does not only concern elected officials since they are subject to it. Members of the Government, members of Parliament, representatives in the European Parliament, holders of local executive functions or elected officials with delegated signature, staff of cabinets, members of independent authorities, holders of jobs or functions at the decision of the Government and appointed by the Council of Ministers as well as the presidents and general managers of a certain number of companies, enterprises, establishments and bodies over which the State exercises total or partial control.

4.4. The Democratic Process

An elected National Parliament is at the heart of any integrity system based on democratic accountability. Its task is formulated thoroughly: to express the sovereign will of the people through the chosen representatives, who assured daily, in their name, that the Executive is accountable for decisions since the liberal on nineteenth-century State.

The relationship between the citizens with the right to vote and the rulers was direct. Therefore, the control that citizens exercised over their leaders was exhausted at the election time. In that state, parties were of little importance. There was still no universal suffrage, but census voting, where only a few could vote. So there was no need for large organizations to articulate and unite interests for political-electoral purposes.

The liberal State characterized by the sharp contrast between the State and Society, by individualism and the atomization of power, and above all by the idea, now put back into circulation, of the minimal or "gendarme" State, the parties were embryonic entities in him or at most parties of notables. Without legal recognition or regulation, these were local associations promoted by candidates for Parliament or by groups of the bourgeoisie that fought for the extension of suffrage or that sometimes represented interest groups.

Such circles grouped a restricted number of people and functioned almost exclusively during electoral periods. The party was a simple provisional machine without any political program, permanent discipline, or organization. The expansion of voting and the democratizing processes of the late nineteenth and early twentieth century's brought the mass parties and the processes of their legal and constitutional recognition. The Party-State is mainly a consequence of mass parties and political struggles for the extension of suffrage and changes in the parliamentary and electoral structure of many European countries.

The notion of the Party-State is of German origin. Some Germanic authors criticise the parliamentary crisis and the deputy's dependence on his party, the so-called imperative mandate in strong discipline for decisions made at the top of the party. The Party-State has supporters and detractors.

Political parties can prevent modern democracies from being moved by emotional and senseless ups and downs making them fall into helplessness, disintegration, and demagoguery. There may be a non-democratic Party-State, but the one that is opposed to the State of privileges or classes. It is a State open to the entire popular community. It has the possibility of defending democracy against demagoguery or other forms of political or social organization, unacceptable for the respect of the rights of individuals. Kelsen understood the Party-State, the general will or the State moves along the line of conciliation between the interests of the different parties.

The parties are organs of the State that demand their constitutionalization to promote their internal democracy. They reject any oligarchic tendency within the party organization. For Radbruch, real democracy is not made up of individuals but parties. The other organs of the State emanate from them. The Party-State, he says, is in the form of the democratic State of our time. Without the mediation of party organization, collective opinion and will would be impossible.

Regarding Schmitt, the Party-State implies that the main political decisions are not taken in Parliament through the exercise of reason and the debate of ideas, but by the party leaders, who oblige their deputies to follow their mandates. The Party-State led Robert Michels to elaborate its famous iron Law of the oligarchy. He refers to the bureaucratization of the party and the absence of internal democracy within it which constitutes, among other things, one of the reasons for the modern discrediting of parties and their so-called crisis.

4.5. The Role of Political Parties

Political science has collected different typologies of parties. The Duverger classification, which distinguishes between single-party, bipartisan and multiparty systems, is famous. This author considers that the types of party systems determine the political system; thus, the one-party system corresponds to the totalitarian or authoritarian State. However, Duverger's classification does not correspond, at times, with the reality of the political system. For example, the People's Republic of China has eight parties, yet it is not a democracy.

Obviously, in liberal democracies, parties perform specific functions that they lack in undemocratic regimes. The functions of parties in democracies have been classified according to two aspects: social and institutional. The first mass parties, which were workers in nature, were in charge of affirming a class identity and preserving and transmitting patterns of behaviour and values that shaped the culture of the working class. According to some party or electoral laws, modern parties continue to have an obligation to promote democratic values, respect for Human Rights, the practice of tolerance, and the right to dissent, as well as to train their members. Members in the ideological principles of the party and disseminate these among citizens.

To carry out such tasks, modern parties usually have the media, publications, cadre schools and, in general, centres for the transmission of their ideas, not only to their members but to all citizens. At present, the socializing role of parties has declined in importance due to the growing role of the non-party media. The partisan media have a precarious existence, as citizens and affiliates prefer less doctrinal information. Those that do have more and more acceptance are the foundations of study, research, and documentation of the parties.

The so-called crisis of the parties has to do with the current weakness of their socializing function. It is interpreted as an inability to link with the aspirations and interests of society. With the crisis in Parliament, which in the classical thesis of liberal democracy was the ideal place for reasoning and informed public (the deputies) to discuss public affairs, the parties? Indeed, it is up to them to allow Civil Society's opinions, views, and criteria to be expressed and subsequently direct them to an effective concretion.

The parties can ensure the generation of opinion movements. However, some critics of the parties have pointed out that they have been overtaken by social movements in their ability to mobilize public opinion. Such censorship must be viewed objectively. Certainly, some parties have lost the capacity to articulate the community's demands. In the face of certain demands from the social movements, they do not act with the required speed.

On the other hand, others update and reformulate their strategies and manage to form better political offers in front of their members and the rest of society in the private and public orders frequented by the new social organizations. Another social function of parties is the representation of interests. Originally, the workers' parties, for example, represented the interests of their class.

Today, parties tend to represent widely varied and sometimes frankly contradictory interests. Moreover, there is a tendency that impels them to configure themselves basically as centrist parties and to qualify their ideological positions, be they left or right. It means that the parties channel multiple interests. Still, they tend to prefer one over the other, considering their historical or ideological origin or a political situation that makes it more profitable to defend certain interests.

The last of the social functions of the parties is their role as legitimators of the political system. The criteria for measuring the legitimacy of a system are multiple. Ranging from its ability to remain stable, be effective and enjoy the acceptance of citizens to respecting Human Rights in all Spheres of Power.

One of the most accepted criteria in a democracy to measure the legitimacy of the system is its capacity to promote democratic procedures and institutions as a whole and guarantee and respect citizens' Fundamental Rights.

The issue of rights and obligations is fundamental. In their external and internal activity, the parties have both in their relations with the State and with other parties. The primary right they have concerning the State is that of their legal recognition, their legal existence, and receiving fair treatment and equal opportunities from the Government and its organs and, on occasions, obtaining public subsidies. The parties' obligations in the external sphere include those of acting through institutional channels, using peaceful means for political struggle, and respecting the rules and democratic procedures in their actions against the rest ofthe parties (Yang, 2020).

Parties have the right to organize freely, since not affecting the fundamental rights of militants or other citizens not violating the Democratic Principles of the Rule of Law. Its primary obligation in the domestic sphere is to respect democracy within it, that is, to have democratic procedures and scrupulously respect the fundamental rights of its members. Suppose the material and immaterial needs of the citizens are not met. In that case, the acceptance of the institutions and the government decreases. Corruption triggers anger, unrest, and ultimately flight. Although flight and displacement are diverse, corruption often also plays a central role. Many people flee from countries where there is no war. Still, unstable structures shape everyday life and worsen the prospects of their residents.

Weak state structures and corrupt institutions are often the starting point for unrest. The stability of a country certainly depends on numerous factors, such as reliable framework conditions, nonviolence, or the Rule of Law (Yang, 2020). However, the connection with corruption can be shown empirically and illustrated with a look at flight statistics: If one compares the number of displaced people with the data from the corruption indices, a clear connection can be seen. The more pronounced the corruption, the more people are fleeing these countries. Therefore, the fight against corruption must be a priority for the international Community when it comes to stabilizing countries and avoiding displacement. To do this, all parties must recognize their role in the process and act accordingly. Developing countries often lack the knowledge to reform their structures. So the developed countries have to support them in the fight against corruption, for example, by orienting development cooperation more specifically towards improving State structures. So far, the disbursement of aid payments has often not been linked to conditions such as the fight against corruption.

Finally, multinational companies also have an important role to play. By observing international guidelines, they can prevent the spread of corruption and thus help stabilize the local economy. Because so far corruption has not harmed the most elite internal democracy is one of the determining issues for democratic life, not exclusively of the parties themselves but a country. Such a democracy goes beyond that practiced at the level of the institutions and organs of the State: it aims to configure an integral democracy that is verified in the State apparatus but also at the level of society and its organizations, at least in the most relevant such as the parties themselves, unions, business organizations, etc.

To calibrate internal democracy, it is necessary to consider at least four elements:

- The level of respect and guarantee of fundamental rights within the party;
- The organization and internal procedures
- The currents within the organization and
- The control bodies of its internal life (Yang, 2020).

4.6. Can Corruption Put Danger in Democracy?

Considered an abuse of power of the elected representatives, political corruption is classically seen as a normal phenomenon because of its sustainability and its useful function in the development of society. Therefore, that crime couldn't be understood as a social pathology.

If this position was acceptable in the 19th century,today, the evolution changes our judgement of corruption. A new concept: Political corruption it is a political virus infecting democracy through the elected official's integrity. This conceptualization enables a new vision of the prevention and control of corruption and tries to estimate the efficiency of the policy against corruption.

As an immemorial evil, inseparable from an imperfect human society corruption, according to the definition of the French Academy, it's an alteration, the act of diverting a person from his duty. Such a definition seems incomplete, retaining only the active component of corruption. It is advisable to add to it the passive component consisting of the one who allows himself to be diverted from his duty by gifts, promises, or persuasion. Corruption is seen as human behaviour involving the intervention of a third party with the prevalence of the particular interest of the agent versus the interest of the principal personal or general interest.

This legal definition in the full extent of the corruptive phenomenon in the common sense of the term:

- Active and passive corruption,
- Favouritism,
- Embezzlement,
- Misappropriation of property,
- Influence peddling.

In short, what some authors have called for several years breach of integrity. That is why conceiving the phenomenon as an abuse of power for private profit. Corruption is "what is legally defined as illegal and what constitutes corruption at the end of a process of negative moral qualification emanating from agents.

Corruption also creates services and products more expensively than necessary or of poorer quality. In addition, not only the quantity but also the quality of public investment suffers because, among other things, spending in the social sector and infrastructure is falling. This hinders the sustainable development of a country and the ability of a government to carry out necessary reforms, for example, for better regulation or faster bureaucracy.

Basic needs of the population, such as access to education or health services, cannot be met as expected. There is a lack of a functioning infrastructure, which is a breeding ground for corruption to preserve these necessary goods - a vicious circle. The dampening effect of corruption can also be seen in alternative welfare indicators, such as general well-being and life satisfaction. Both are significantly less pronounced in countries affected by corruption than in comparatively corruption-free countries.

About Bribing

One must not participate in any way in acts of bribery involving government officials(including public officials of any level or employees of public sector entities) to obtain an unfair advantage. As University officials, must not participate in acts of corruption that include bribes or kickbacks to another company or person to obtain an unfair advantage. Also, must not request or accept bribes or kickbacks from third parties. In these events, must immediately inform our supervisor or the Compliance Officer. Some examples of bribery originate for the following purposes:

- Get preferential treatment concerning taxes payable or customs.
- Obtain permits or approvals from regulators.
- Elude the laws and regulations applicable to the University.
- Intervene in the assignment of a contract or some commercial transactions. From the social point of view, corruption has been installed as a determining factor in the scenarios of extreme poverty that large proportions of the planet suffer.

Likewise, the conflicts between the various social hierarchies and their involvement in struggles for power and personal benefits have shown the need to rethink the different social strata's structure, relationship, and distance. The ethnic question has also been permeable to corruption, fuelling racial conflicts in many countries. To better conceptualize this facet of corruption, the literature gives a predominant role to the transparency of information and the strengthening of interpersonal trust to strengthen the social bond between the different actors.

The myth of culture Corruption is a phenomenon that alters or disrupts the shape of something. But it can refer to material or moral realities, which is why several senses of the term appear that help us to specify our object. There is corruption of material things and other forms of corruption of moral actions. In this definition, we observe a reflection on the ethical and material planes of the phenomenon.

We will not focus on material issues because we believe that corruption is based on the actors' actions. When trying to define the phenomenon, special attention should be paid to the agent's position. Therefore, corruption in those acts will constitute the active or passive violation of a duty.

Positional or non-fulfilment of any specific function performed within the discretion framework to obtain any extra-positional benefit, whatever its nature. In this case, we observe a concern for the agent and the transgression concerning a certain normative framework. Depending on the subject of corruption, initiating corruption relations:

- Requesting (extortion) bribes at the initiative of an official.
- Bribery initiated by the petitioner. Depending on the subject of corruption, who is the bribe-giver:
- An individual bribe (from a citizen)
- A business bribe (from a legal firm)
- Criminal bribery (by criminal entrepreneurs - for example, the drug mafia).

The level of corruption in Germany, as well as in other countries, is usually judged by two indicators. One is the annual rating of perceptions of this problem, compiled by the international non-governmental organization Transparency International (TI) based on surveys and expert assessments. Unlike Transparency International, the Federal Office for Criminal Cases is not engaged in subjective assessments of the level of corruption in Germany but rather specific corrupt officials.

The problem is, the detectives explain, that both the persons involved in the corruption deal - the one who gives and the one who takes a bribe - are criminals. And unlike ordinary criminality, here, as a rule, no innocent victim is willing to go to the police. Exaggerating the public and private division regarding certain actors' behaviours can be a misleading practice since public activity is very difficult to isolate from private activity.

The market and the State have multiple interconnections. However, due to theoretical needs, they are separated, it must be recognized that in reality, they function overlapping. So, it is not an appropriate decision to separate the morality of the private sector from that which can be observed in the public sector, and the two explain the whole. The private is linked to organized crime or illegal acts of individuals, and the public relates to those illegal practices that affect the efficiency of the government.

Numerous fraudulent bankruptcies of companies or the emptying of the same by their managers - with the consequent damage they cause to the economy; or where their leaders have used certain political parties or unions as private property, leading them to collapse regardless of the wear and tear they caused to the democratic system.

For classical political theory, reflection on corruption is not a new topic from ancient Greece. Through renaissance and modernity, they are deviation from the pure forms of government. Of its objective of the common good, it was considered a clear indication of corruption. In modern times, and with the distinction between what is public and what is private, political thinking around corruption focused on those individual actions that used public goods for their benefit.

Political reflection on corruption covers a wide spectrum of issues ranging from political systems and institutional structure, Power, centralization, and decentralization, democratic consolidation, to the size of the State and legitimacy of governments (Gorta, 2016).

In general terms, the greatest effect of political corruption, refers to political reasons and effects, which is different from political corruption. This concept is not defined in work, is the impotence and incapacity of the State. In short, political corruption, in most cases, prevents a political community from achieving its goals. The appearance of corruption triggers a series of processes that tend to develop corrupt vicious circles that feed themselves if not dealt with in time. In these conditions, a rarefied climate of insecurity arises that erodes the bonds of interpersonal trust and those existing between citizens and the institutions and powers of the State (Gorta, 2016).

These conditions undermine the government's legitimacy in power while discrediting the entire political issue itself. One of the reasons for the low corruption found in Finland is precisely the collective and collegiate decision-making structure that the country has. In this author's thinking, collegiate forms are praised as difficult to corrupt if the majority of their members are convinced of certain Ethical Values. For this reason, the collegiate decision has been a tradition in Finland since the 17th century. There is a double control system in public bodies. Studies suggest that the condition for the federal structure not to engender a new type of corruption that is more difficult to control is the non-fragmentation of the system. The State in decentralization does not neglect implementing specific corruption controls in the new structures. Other authors have devoted themselves to research on the effects of political and administrative decentralization on the phenomenon of corruption (Gorta, 2016).

Political decentralization, which consists of giving regions more autonomy so they can legislate in areas whose jurisdiction was the central government, increases corruption. However, the same study indicates that decentralization, which implies greater autonomy over public spending, would reduce corruption.

Along the same lines are some authors who affirm that a federal-type State contributes to creating a more honest and efficient government through the competence of the different provinces and jurisdictions. Research in this area provides a greater number of elements to judge the totality of the problem, as evidenced by the increasing publication of works in this regard (Gorta, 2016).

Corruption is functional for politics insofar as it facilitates the functioning of political systems and can help a regime sustain itself or adapt successfully. As an alternative to the functionalist argument, the different types of relationships between people and groups that corruption tends to create. The author proposes a matrix with the following analysis variables: integrating or disintegrating the group's practices and; stability or temporary instability of the group over time (Gorta, 2016).

Societies positively assessed corruption as a mechanism that unblocked the rigidities of systems that resisted change. At the time, these systems were conservative patrimonial and resisted incorporating political innovations. In this context, Huntington imagines a certain positive functionality of corruption. Still, from there, to extrapolate this thought to a permanent recommendation on corruption as a beneficial instrument, there is a great distance. Latin American experiences show that corruption so affronts the political system that it undermines the institutional foundations and degrades interpersonal trust if it is not countered. Bribes made to officials by potential contractors cause contracts, both from the government and privatized State-owned companies, not to be assigned to the most efficient contractor but to the one willing to a higher bribe. The causes of the consequent inefficiency in the performance of the contractor's work are many: the most efficient contractor may feel scrupulous about engaging in fraudulent practices and therefore refrain from participating in the bidding process; he who assumes the payment of a bribe will hope to obtain subsidies, monopoly profits and less and less strict regulations; projects can become more complex and challenging to carry out as bribes are easier to disguise; to compensate the payment of the bribe, the successful bidder may lower the quality of his service or the quality of the materials to be used to carry out the work; Proceedings can be dramatically delayed to obtain even higher bribery payments.

In the framework of an economy with signs of corruption, there is an increase in transaction costs for the private sector caused not only by bribes but also due to the intentional delays in carrying out business projects. Corruption favours the unfair distribution of income since, to compensate for the losses caused by badly assigned contracts, higher taxes are charged, reducing spending on matters of public need. In addition to concluding that corruption generates income disparity (based on the study of the Gini coefficient in several countries), other authors also affirm that education and the distribution of land are equally affected. (Gorta, 2016).

Along the same lines, the researchers found evidence that spending on education, health, maintenance, and operations areas is reduced by corruption. In these areas, it is more complicated than decision-makers budgets can get a "slice of the cake."

4.7. The Relationship between State, Market, and the Public Sector

Despite national and regional peculiarities and differences in political, economic, and cultural systems The Vienna Declaration and Program of Action (1993) aim to guide States on the respect, protection, and fulfilment of Human Rights and stress that they should be implemented fairly and equitably worldwide. The UN and OECD Guiding Principles, the ILO Tripartite Declaration, and other general guidelines reinforce these principles and encourage States to establish national Human Rights mechanisms.

One of these methods is responsive regulation. Organizations are encouraged to voluntarily comply with Human Rights and Environmental Laws and standards. When they violate these rules, the State must sanction them, guarantee recourse to victims and avoid repeated abuses.

States cannot control activities in other States; they are expected to create mechanisms to ensure that organizations receiving State support in their territory respect Human Rights abroad.

• This tool refers to the link between the State and economic activities, covering the main aspects of the State's Human Rights obligations when interacting with economic actors.

• It also includes guidelines published by national, European, or international institutions, which promote respect for Human Rights and guidelines focusing on the link between State entities and economic activities (Burdett, 2012).

Tools intended for the State when it acts as an economic actor to avoid that related activities negatively impact Human Rights. These activities vary, the most common public procurement, privatization processes, public-private partnerships (PPP), concession contracts, or contracts linked to the energy performance policy. Tools are intended for the State when it creates or concludes company agreements with private organizations (state-owned companies, commonly known as state-owned enterprises). As owner and/or controller, the State must verify whether its activities comply with Human Rights rules and standards.

Usually, State-owned enterprises are accountable to the State entity to which they are linked. That entity, in turn, has enhanced jurisdiction to oversee their activities. This close monitoring should, in principle, include respect for Human Rights (Burdett, 2012). Tools intended for the State when it intervenes in the economy by granting economic incentives to private organizations, such as labels, preferential credits, insurance for activities in third countries, subsidies, licenses, incentives for target programs like circular economic projects, etc.

The State is expected to provide enhanced monitoring and create mechanisms to prevent the recipients of such incentives from adversely affecting Human Rights through their activities. Some of the mechanisms used by the State to identify risks, monitor compliance, or remedy deficiencies or deficiencies are listed below in a non-exhaustive manner.

4.8. Lobbies as a Pressure Instrument

Lobbies come from various horizons: NGOs, religious associations, employees unions, employer representatives, or even local communities. The data on which the assessment of the importance of lobbies is based are approximate. In that case, those representing the interests of companies far outperform others in terms of numbers, budgets, and employees. But measuring the real influence of lobbies on public decision-making comes up against many methodological difficulties (Mantaluta, 2019). Only from the 1980sthe terms lobbying were used in economic and sociological literature. The subject of debate, the generally accepted definition, presents lobbies as groups seeking to influence Power.

The definitions of lobbies differ from political parties insofar as they do not present candidates for elections and do not seek to conquer the direct exercise of Power. Some definitions do not include administrative agencies or bodies of civil servants, and most exclude social movements.

The European Union incorporates employee unions as an interest group in its transparency register. Rigorously analyzing lobbying requires getting rid of preconceptions that partially reflect reality.

Without denying the existence of illegal practices buying scientists, bribing politicians, etc., lobbying practices are much broader than those most visible in the media. Even if a part of their activities remains invisible to the eyes of the sociologist, ethnographic investigators have managed to conduct interviews with employees of lobbies to talk about their professional activity (Mantaluta, 2019).

Because rather than overriding the Law as common sense might suggest, the lobbies opt for fine strategies, which make it possible to modify the latter. Lobbies are commonly denounced as exercising powerful control over public decisions, ethnographic observation shows that their very existence is not taken for granted by lobbyists.

Therefore, part of the working time of lobbyists' employees consists of convincing their clients of their usefulness, calling into question the idea of their omnipotence. The number of lobbies is subject to caution and probably underestimated. The penalties for failure to comply with the obligation to register are not very dissuasive. Certain groups are exempt from it, such as religious associations.

Measuring their actual contribution to decision-making is even more difficult. It is first of all possible to take an interest in the lobbies' budget because of the EU transparency register. Compare the 40 million Euros of Cefic, representing the interests of the European chemical industry, with that of Greenpeace, one of the largest NGOs in the EU, but with only 1.7 million Euros, gives an idea of the importance of each of these two lobbies.

This solution makes it possible to give an appreciable measure of the weight of the lobbies. Still, it presents two difficulties: The declared budgets can again be the subject of under-declaration, and secondly it considers the means and not actual results (Mantaluta, 2019).

Market regulation does not emanate from a benevolent State that pursues collective well-being but from the meeting between a demand and a supply of regulation emanating from actors rationally pursuing their private interest. The demand for regulation comes from companies in a branch.

Regulation is often preferred over other forms of State support - pricing, subsidies - because it only benefits firms already in the market and weakens competition. For example, licenses constitute a barrier to entry into certain markets, and their establishment or strengthening may favour the sector's players (Mantaluta,2019). Thus there is a basic difference in the engagement inherent in each of the two groups.

Pressure groups seek power to politically influence the conduct of society without being directly in power. In contrast, interest groups seek to have a voice in politics. Lobbies would be nothing more than actions of pressure groups that organize capital, material, and information in an attempt to influence governmental decisions without becoming political parties. Groups of interest are the gender and the initial state of the societal disposition in search of political voice.

Pressure groups are the most advanced state of a functional organization that uses an instrument to give the demands, which is the lobby (Mantaluta, 2019). It is important to consider how pressure groups are formed from three theories (group theory, rational choice theory, and agency theory).

• The first theory is the group theory. To better understand the theme, we will adopt the concept of which group is equivalent to the sum of activities elaborated by people who aim to reach a common goal.

They are people who jointly expand their efforts in achieving a satisfactory result of what they have set out to do. In political science, the first systematic organization of group theory occurred in the early twentieth century, around 1908,afterArthur Bentley published the book entitled "The Process of Government" (Zak, 2019). For Bentley, man would be an animal with rational interests. Life is for this animal as a set of conflicting interests. It becomes necessary to use techniques to give security to everyday human relations. He says that the meaning and organization of a society can be understood as a mosaic of interest groups in reciprocal interaction.

This would lead to constant conflicts between groups seeking to maximize interests. In the existence of groups that seek to maximize their interests the Government of different origins and interests that in an electoral panorama in cyclical periods, is a regulator of the struggles of corporate groups (Zak, 2019).

Pressure groups present themselves as a range of behaviours motivated to solve problems of a group, general or specific, influencing the decision-making power in the pursuit of collective lawsuits. The theory of groups is based on the association of people. It is important to affirm the need to articulate the groups in search of favourable outcomes to the needs presented because ofthe inherent set ofinterests in the political world (Uk, 2019).

• The second theory regarding the formation of pressure groups is the Theory of Rational Choice. Initially, it emphasizes that it tends to justify how the interaction of individuals constructs models of social action and the interactions of these models explain the diversity of the diverse groups. Institutions of greater importance, forming the foundation of society since the interaction of institutions and economic theories would result in rules to be obeyed by society establishing relations of balance to the economic and social system, giving human interactions.

The relationships presented come from the oppositions in the positions and preferences of each individual that, with dialogue, create values that allow the creation of diverse social groupings (Zak, 2019). In this way, individuals would have their behaviour affected by institutions, but they would also influence political situations. In the confrontation between bureaucrats, political agents, and pressure groups, institutions would play a primary role in designing thematic areas of dispute. They would define winners and losers.

The Rational Choice theory has simplicity on its axioms based on individualism and collectivism. The person seeks to satisfy their needs to achieve their well-being. At that moment, the lobby is inserted as a mechanism of associative organization. The pressure groups take the opportunity to insert them (Zak, 2019).

• The third theory of lobby formation is the Agency Theory which aims to demonstrate the relationship between private and public interest. The agency contributes to unravelling the behaviour of politicians and public agents in decision-making regarding public policies. For him, the main axis is the desire to potentiate the person's usefulness. Public conduct focuses on the role of "agents," who are the "top" delegates who run a business. The interest of the subjects falls on the contracts that can be signed between the agent (= principal) and executor (= delegate).

It is clear the existence of an asymmetry in the relation because it is not always obtained what is contracted. It deals with human conduct subject to unethical, perhaps criminal behaviour (Zak, 2019). Certain deviations from conduct can be perceived in situations involving Powers of the Republic, considering the regulatory power of the Executive before what was legislated by the National Parliament.

Given the opening of the law issued, public and political agents may distort the norm's function in the legal system in situations of issuance of decrees and regulations, in which the executive branch (regulatory agencies) exceed its jurisdiction, there is a possibility of suspending acts to preserve the public interest. In this context, the theory of analysis is critical because the lobbyist is an agent that acts within the "main" subject, which is the pressure group.

Despite having similarities with the people's representative, the relationship between public servants and the main issue has differences since there is no contract between them (Zak, 2019). The political agent is expected to represent the interests of citizens who have placed their trust in that person for an elective term. At the same time, lobbyists seek to interfere in the decision-making process.

4.9. Lobbying x Corruption x Influence Traffic

American and foreign, who consider how political decisions are formed in the United States, find it challenging to recognize the lesser value and the most minor positive function of lobbying in a democratic society. Some would equate lobbying with bribery and corruption. A recent opinion poll revealed deep dissatisfaction with the role played by interest groups in the United States. Special interests exert too much influence on government action (Zak, 2019).

For over 71%, interest groups have too much power, only 8.4%felt that they "don't have enough power There isn't an alternative to the current open system of intervention in public policy if we want to keep the freedom of speech among the fundamental rights and claim against what we have to complain about. In the Federalist Papers of 1787, James Madison explained that the Federation of States would be a safeguard against factions and the risks of insurgency.

Lobbying in the United States is thus based on the well-established right of citizens to petition the government that the wrongs suffered have recovered. This fundamental right has fostered the development of large, complex, and diverse interest groups, which seem to function efficiently in the American context. This facility is explained by the fragmented nature of the political system:

- It offers a variety of points of access to interest groups.
- It can also be presented by the ideological pluralism within each political party.
- It is almost an alternative to the decline of citizen participation in its other modalities, particularly voting. In democratic systems, one of the goals of the deliberative activity of citizens and their representatives is the discovery and implementation of a common good. Public policies are part of a process, fallible but capable of self-correction, through

which ordinary citizens and their elected representatives manage to discern what is good for them (Zak, 2019).

In American society, the pluralism of (group) interests offers multiple opportunities to represent the diversity of citizens, allowing free competition in the marketplace of ideas and causes. This pluralism leads to a timely dispersion of political power and action means. It promotes negotiation, debate, compromise.

Today, this place is given to lobbying ultimately involves much more than the pressure exerted on political decision-makers to vote in one direction or another on the occasion of a law. It includes research and analysis, observation, efforts to disseminate information and arouse public interest. It involves setting up joint actions aimed at the "education;' so to speak, of three main groups: public opinion, members of interest groups, and political decision-makers. Lobbyists try to consider all the impacts that a political decision could have. If they do not seek to assert all these aspects themselves, they at least aim to know the other parties' arguments to be able to take them into account (Zak, 2019).

Lobbying is not just about communicating directly to decision-makers. It is the smallest part of lobbyists' activity. Here are some of the arguments put forward for lobbying contribution to the democratic process in the United States: Lobbying results in the creation of intermediary organizations between the individual and mass society. It leads to establishing interest "groups" where those concerned can debate and listen to one another on important issues.

It can lead to coalitions of shared interests, transcending ideologies and partisan politics, in pursuit of common pragmatic goals. New groups of citizens thus participate effectively in developing public policies (Dutt, 2010). Interest groups offer's alternative modes of empowerment - not only for the best-placed elites and commercial actors but also for those who seek to be the voice of the voiceless.

Such a culture allows a wide variety of interest groups to engage in strategy, discover how the administration works, and participate in the preparation of decisions (Dutt, 2010). It also calls for the development of an unlimited number of diverse interests. Such a culture is in harmony with the idea that politics demand recognition ofthis diversity.

Lobbying can help groups fit into this perspective through skills, insights, information about how politics is formed. This positive conception of lobbying reflects a vision of the political space marketplace: a system that corrects itself, where transparency and accountability are the only suitable means of achieving political goals. Most of those in the lobbying profession in the United States agree that honesty is the best policy. Suppose a lobbyist is known to be dishonest and deceptive. In that case, decision-makers will stop trusting him and be sidelined. With new technologies, lobbying can lead to even more openness, accessibility, and decentralization of decision-making processes (Dutt, 2010).

More people can be better informed in terms of political analysis and the themes to be developed to influence the policy. Specific lobbying actions can be harmful: campaigns are conducted dishonestly, using rigged instruments, discreetly. Special interests enjoy political privileges that are not democratically accounted for.

The question arises in particular in the case of the financing of political campaigns, leading to backlash between politicians and lobbyists, and in the case of triangular exchanges between government, business circles, and military establishment. Backyard arrangements that are not transparent to the public cause a high degree of political corruption. However, for many critics, the real problem is not so much this kind of corrupt lobbying but a subtle distortion of the democratic process. Many feel that lobbying has excessive influence, that producers are better represented in the system than consumers, that narrow special economic interests are better than consumers. And suppose the new communication technologies allow a more decentralized and transparent promotion action. In that case, the best equipped and financed groups are well placed to take advantage of these technologies, even to use them in a deceptive way (Dutt, 2010).

4.10. The Advisers

This type of professional exercises the activity does not hold a specific academic formation; that is, what determines whether a person is capable of activity is their ability to absorb, organize, and redirect information about their academic background. Many advisors began to act almost by chance because they have an easy way of dealing with the public and because they have a high persuasion. Many of these professionals previously in public agencies usually use their contacts, influence, and friendships to carry out their work. However, it requires more than good contacts because "there is no use having good contacts if there is nothing to communicate to the decision-maker" (Godwin, 2012).

When so many interests combine to weigh on decision-making bodies and to shape the information necessary for discussion, aren't decision-makers tempted to give up the effort to educate themselves and their collaborators on the issues under debate? Do they not trust this global education action which would result from the very game of competition between groups? Decision-makers then sacrifice their duty of objectivity and informed judgment to benefit a simple balancing of competing interests. It's believed that too much focus on interest groups weakens ordinary citizens' desire to participate in political life.

The system is now only at the service of the noisy elites. Finally, given the increasing cost of lobbying campaigns, it is increasingly likely that the poor and the voiceless have less and less representation and access to this policy formation process (Godwin, 2012). Democracy is the worst regime invented by men, apart from all the others. - Winston Churchil Lobbying is one of the faces of this paradox: the American system of interest groups is very accessible, but it also conceals enormous potential for non-democracy. Mass movements continue to have a voice, but we are witnessing a growing marginalization of the voiceless.

In the United States, stricter lobbying regulation would be the only way to limit abuse and keep it open to the good. In a free society, there will never be a perfect system for promoting political causes. It is to be expected that even with the implementation of new regulations, such as the McCain-Feingold law of 2002, new holes new workaround strategies will emerge. They will require new measures to hunt abuses and regulate (Godwin, 2012).

Interest group politics and lobbying are undoubtedly inevitable in a democratic society. But Moral reflection and professional Ethics must at least serve as remedies and prevent corruption. We propose the Woodstock Principles for Ethical Conduct in Lobbying as a framework for intervention to promote public policy interests (Godwin, 2012). These principles are divided into seven sections:

- Lobbying and Common good;
- The relationship between the lobbyist and his client;
- The relationship between the lobbyist and the policymaker;
- Lobbyists and public opinion formers; • When there is a conflict of interest;
- Lobbying strategy and tactics;
- Integrity of the lobbyist profession.

5. Reform of the State

5.1. Introduction

The Reform of the State process implies modifications in budgetary aspects, distribution of tasks, new forms of work, new organizational structures, etc., to obtain adequate and efficient results meeting the population needs. This task constitutes a true challenge that transcends the political colour of the day, pursuing the entire community's well-being as its sole purpose. Likewise, it implies the training of human resources and the achievement of the cohesion of organizational and individual objectives, providing transparency in management and combating corruption.

The process of change is a complex path that encounters many obstacles, especially the resistance of the dependents themselves. Organizational culture, leadership styles, and structure are examples of potential difficulties in advancement. Will it be possible just to attend to political interests and international compromises to reform the State?

5.2. Gradual Decentralization

Historically, reform policy should not only consider the problems it intends to solve but also identify the paths that the administration should take to best respond to its missions. The search for better productivity and public satisfaction inevitably requires an increase in qualifications, a re-motivation of civil servants, and the elimination of unprofitable jobs within a general framework of administrative reorganization. But to achieve it, the administrative reform must be part of a movement of de-politicization of the public service, which operates by a separation between the political and the administrative. It involves systematic, continuous, and effective evaluation of programs. In the 21st century, the missions of the State evolved according to the needs of the population. New professions - inconceivable only a few years ago - have arisen at an accelerated pace; the professions of civil servants are evolving rapidly under the combined effect of several factors, namely the broadening of their social purpose, the change in internal and external relational modes of collaboration, the appearance of new technologies, the need for various qualifications in previously services. In this rapidly changing environment, the quality of the public service is assessed based on its ability to adapt to the needs expressed locally and to its assessment (Vishwakarma, 2021).

The archaic structures of the Administration pose serious problems that any reform must take into account. The Administration suffers from almost empty structures. Almost all were created more than forty-five years ago and have not seen any evolution, modest modernization, little updating, no adaptation in the objectives to be achieved. And even less at the level of working instruments. In addition, the diversification of State functions has also increased the number of ministries. The creation of a ministry and a certain number of services and their attachment to a particular ministry are most often determined by decisions taken according to the political situation.

Addressing this issue is imperative that current governments address as a priority. For the latter, modernization, therefore, means revising the spirit of the standards that organize the missions of the public service and the structures of the administrative units responsible for promoting this service.

The competition, according to Bernard Chenot, is a complex operation but relatively easy to interpret because, in reality, the competition process seeks to combine a principle of Public Interest which is the selection organized in the interest of the Public Service, with the principle of respect for citizens' rights, namely the rule of equality for all in access to public employment.

5.2.1. Components of a Public Administration Program

A complete and adequate description of the components of a program is essential to assess its implementation. Components are:

- Strategies,
- Activities,
- Behaviours,
- Ways of communication and
- Technologies for the implementation of the program and the specification of the beneficiaries, and where the implementation takes place.

Discomforts and tensions resulting from the administration and its functioning often stem from the public's ignorance and the administration of their rights and duties. The idea that the administration is available to the public must always be brought to the mind of the public servant (Vishwakarma,2019).

This is why the mission of any administrative institution is to pass on, from one generation to the next, not only know-how but also Ethics. Training is an essential element of valuing professional skills, upgrading skills of adaptability and efficiency. Admittedly, the number of civil servants has increased in specific units due to the development of administrative action and political pressure and the desire to secure clientele.

There is a clear relationship between the development and number of agents and intervention of politicians in the administration. It should also be noted that the politicians who complain about the overabundance of civil servants in specific sectors are precisely the same people who are at the origin of their recruitment.

The sociologist Max Weber had emphasized the importance of the specification of functions by foreseeing the existence - in the legal -

rational domination - of a bureaucracy subordinated to an authority fixing the competencies and the attributions.

5.2.2. Fight against corruption and upgrading of the salaries of civil servants

The shortcomings of the administrative machine efficiency and performance are a source of discontent for the public and public officials. They are the target of criticism levelled at them. We often tend to consider that there is in the administration a regrettable slowness, incompetence, a lack of initiative, and notorious creativity; civil servants suffer from a lack of recognition.

The public sector faces more and more competition from jobs in the private sector, especially as these are much more remunerative. So public servants almost everywhere feel bitterness when they see the imbalance between what they perceive and what their counterparts in the private sector get. This difference in remuneration in the two sectors is explained by the fact that the income of a civil servant changes, during his career, according to the advancements he obtains. The organization of public employment in Lebanon follows the principle of hierarchy. The latter helps to define the course of labour. Whatever the level of his responsibility, the civil servant is part of this hierarchy, at the top of which is the minister. He, therefore, participates in a collective public service task that constantly calls for the combination of several qualities, including integrity, discretion, efficiency, and loyalty in the performance of his missions.

5.2.3. Relations between political power and administration

Max Weber seemed to establish a separation between the administration "in charge of carrying out orders" and the political body having recourse to physical and legitimate coercion. This separation constitutes the primary mechanism of the functioning of any administrative apparatus. It was up to the politicians sitting in Parliament or in the cabinet (Government) to decide the policy.

At the same time, it was incumbent on the civil servants to carry out the orders of their political superiors without them ever being entrusted with functions related to policymaking. Separation - understood in the sense of not confusing political power and administration - is the surest way for the administration to continue to serve political Power.

The administration, writes Gerard Timsit, cannot be linked to the latter, "under penalty, at the same time as the political power placed at the head of the State would change, of having to be, too, renewed in its totality": A strict separation between political power and the administration is inconceivable because all the various bodies and services ensure the execution of decisions emanating from higher authorities. This execution is manifested by the interpretation of the texts, the search for means of performance, adapting means to the circumstances to achieve the objectives set in the decisions taken by the political superiors.

5.2.4. Assessment of results

Here, results consist of immediate results, results (impacts), and the medium-term results (effects) for the long term. For the evaluation, use impact indicators for measuring the long-term results related to the objectives of the program and output indicators to measure the immediate and medium-term results. The output indicators measure the effects of the program: on the target population as a whole.

Set up of the program. In the first case, should be raised two types of output indicators, with research in the field or the help of databases and/ or existing entries:

• Degree of global coverage:

• Criteria to a rate of coverage of the target population. Both the deficit and the surplus of people benefiting are the reasons for changes in the route. The first demonstrates the need for expansion, and second that there is a waste of resources (non-eligible as target population are benefiting);

• Degree of coverage varies from the program Measures the participation of different subgroups of the target population proposal. This rate can portray the discrimination (or bias) in the selection of clients of the program depending on Region, age, sex, etc... The second point, i.e., the evaluation of results to program users, can be used to measure indicators of benefits, which take into account the specific objectives of each program or project.

Rob Vos (1993) gives some examples of indicators most commonly used among users of the program and target population:

1) For programs of nutrition - malnutrition rates by age, mortality, and morbidity;

2) For programs of education - illiteracy rates, the repetition, of evasion; coefficients of schooling and degrees of education;

3) To programs of health - mortality rates in general, child mortality, maternal mortality, and birth, of fertility and life expectancy at birth;

4) For housing programs - quantitative deficit for housing, housing construction quality, and availability of essential services. The indicators show the input means or the resources available to achieve the objectives. Scarce resources are inadequate (in financial terms, labour, equipment, etc.). Almost always tend to undermine the expected results.

The rational components of the administrative program constitute an ambitious and coherent whole and an unprecedented advance in the right of citizens to have a competent administration performing its tasks effectively and attentive to their concerns. However, the fate of this Reform is linked to the will of the political power in place. On the other hand, this Reform should be accompanied by a change in the citizen's mentality. The latter had lost belief in the ability of administrative institutions to meet his aspirations.

Public services often appear to citizens as complex machinery that requires them to go through a maze of formalities without always having the certainty of getting an answer. The decline in the administration's capacity is fuelling the discontent of the population not only in the cities and among the better-off citizens but especially among the disadvantaged people.

Administrators need the norms and values that legitimize their position and facilitate the citizens'. On the other hand, successful socialization encourages the acceptance of constraints; the citizen persuades himself to obey standards of general interest. Therefore, it is up to the State's duty to guide and strengthen the citizen in morality to ensure the administrative function in the service of the nation. Thus, when the man is assured of his material and moral needs, he becomes immune to his morality against necessity and corruption. Whatever the improvements made to the administration, the administrative order would have no duration without amoral reform through organizational socialization. The new relations between the administration and the citizen consist of redistributing resources equally or equitably among all. To bring the citizen the networks of public services into direct contact so that the latter the citizens can find most of the essential public services that need.

To achieve the objectives, it is necessary to act in two directions:

• Throughout the territory, the existing public services networks should be better used. • A new network should be created in rural or urban areas where public services appear insufficient. Thus, only a functional administration of services will allow the State to be reconciled with the citizen.

5.2.5. Regional Development

Like any other system, a socio-economic system is characterized by a systemic quality. A system is a set of objects and processes called components, interconnected and interacting with each other, which form a single whole. The Region's economy is characterized by cumulative effects, consistently increasing the concentration of population and production in the region.

The concentration of several enterprises of the same industry in the cities raises the total demand of this industry for the corresponding factors of production, for example, for procurement raw materials, electricity, etc. As a result, a sufficiently extensive sales market appears, corresponding to intermediate products, which can stimulate the location of an enterprise for the production of intermediate products in the cities.

The production complex is formed by industries (enterprises) due to activities, which are tangible products and production infrastructure. The social complex includes industries that provide living conditions for the population: trade, public catering, public services for the population, culture, housing, communal services, etc. Large cities' industrial and social complexes are the main users of territorial resources: labour, natural, and financial. Thus, a region is socio-economic spatial integrity characterized by the structure of production, the presence of all forms of ownership, the concentration of the population, jobs, the spiritual life of a person, with local government bodies. Large cities, as a rule, have a diversified structure of the economy.

The basis of their competitive advantages is the connection, often unique, in one geographic point of a favourable location, good (for their Region) transport links, and social and industrial infrastructure potential. The critical role of a large city in the Region's economy is also determined by the fact that it is on its territory that financial and commodity markets are mostly concentrated. Here decisions are formed that determine the entire course of economic life. The economically active Region is a kind of intermediary between consumers, producers, and government bodies. In many situations, the city acts as an independent economic agent, making decisions and carrying out business operations related to the corresponding costs and revenues. This circumstance leads to the commonality of interests of various economic entities operating in the city:

- Business circles (business).
- Hired workers presenting an offer on the labour market localized in the city and at the same time being consumers in the markets for final products localized here.
- Owners of urban real estate, acting as full-fledged representatives in the market for residential and industrial premises and at the same time consumers of the final product.

6. National Defence

The National Defence is liable for the conservation and coherence of the popularity-based State of Law known today. The political help of society is fundamental for the National Defence since the population is equipped to affect the arrangement and advancement of public strategies. Rulers and lawmakers also tend to leave this matter a little aside.

Despite the lack of interest on the subject by both the population and elected officials, the Nation's Defence shouldn't be treated lightly. The National Defence gives continuity to the State and institutions, protects resources, and guarantees the State's Sovereignty. The Sovereignty that is taken as the legal rationalization of the Power of command, that is, it is the legitimating of the coercive Power of the State.

Sovereignty is closely linked to National Defence. Without Sovereignty, there would be no independence of the State to rule over its territory, its people, to create its laws and make its decisions in international relations independently and following the population's interests. Article 2 of the United Nations Charter about the international respect for the Sovereignty of the UN member States and non-interference in the internal affairs of States guarantees the people exclusive authority to establish rules within their Country (Gill, 2012).

National Defence is as vital to the Nation as education and health and about ensuring the continuity of the democratic institutions of the State, protecting the resources used and the knowledge created by the society of that country. It is mainly a matter of maintaining public order for the population.

In addition, the National Defence also has the function of preserving the Nation's protecting Nation interests abroad, preserving the integrity of people over its jurisdiction, and contributing to Peace and Security. Security is defined as the relative condition of collective and individual protection of the members of society against threats to its survival and autonomy.

National Security provides the main justification for exercising Sovereignty and the monopoly on the legitimate use of means of force (Gill,2012). The Security defined here does encompass not only traditional military issues but also political, social, and economic issues that may pose a threat to the country.

Therefore, National Defence, Sovereignty, and Security are interconnected. The first one aims to preserve and protect the last two, the second offers the guarantee of autonomy within the international Community, and the latter guarantees the legitimacy of the first two. The National Defense Policy outlines the guidelines to be followed to achieve the desired security state. A Nation needs a culture of Defence.

The National Interest is understood as the need for Security that each State has within the constant changes of international relations to decide how best to act to resolve its internal issues autonomously (Gill, 2012). He says that it is necessary, consequently, that each country should provide its internal and external Security by developing Military Power, a Diplomatic activity, and an Intelligence Service.

Diplomacy has a very important role in the peaceful negotiation of conflict resolution between nations. If the litigation cannot be solved by any means other than the use of force, there are the country's armed forces.

The Intelligence Service promotes the collection and analysis of data to support policymakers. In addition, the concept of National Defence is sometimes confused with its military organization, that is, the defence made by the army, navy, and aeronautics. However, there is not necessarily an interrelationship between Defence and the use of armed force. Still, it is correct to say that in extreme cases and as a last resort, its application becomes fundamental for a State to defend itself against external aggressions.

Defence is the activity developed to guarantee the Security of the Sovereignty of the State and its population as a proper instrument. New actors come on the scene to defend their interests, such as diplomats who always seek to achieve the Nation's goals internationally and in an entirely peaceful manner (Gill, 2012).

It is of vital importance for the Nation to have a Security of the State to guarantee security and public order for the population, having multidisciplinary capacities interconnected and instrumented through a system of guidelines to be followed.

The politically determined National Defence Policy is also important to protect State assets and interests inside and outside the national territory. Analyzing National Defence in this way relates to the country's Security inside and outside its territory, including several other factors (already cited) that not only the Armed Forces. For the maintenance of this, Security is generated, by the government, public policies of Defence. These policies are often based on university studies and the research and analysis of information made by government intelligence agencies (Gill, 2012).

6.1. National Security

Security can be a relative condition of protection in which it can neutralize perceptible acts with the existence of someone or something with a reasonable expectation of success. A safe and secure organization is achieved through standards and protection for defined sets of information, systems, facilities, communications, personnel, equipment, or operations.

Protective measures should retain some proportionality in perceived threats, their existence, effectiveness, and autonomy of who - or what - is being protected. In the absence of proportionality, the pursuit of Security becomes the effectiveness, autonomy, and, in the limit, the very existence of the "object" of the protection (Gibler,2010).

The proportionality requirement is a tricky point in the notion of safety while an absolute condition of the existence of a measure or method of uncertainty. The total protection of everything and/or of all, against everything and/or all, is something not impossible in an intellectual and psychological perspective, but the more undesirable is totalitarian Security.

Security of the State acts through a policy that anticipates internal and external tendencies that may put national projects at risk, safeguarding the Freedom, Human Rights, and Security of Nation citizens. This approach transcends the classic concept of National Security, which favours conventional threats of a political-military nature, through a multidimensional approach that considers the various dimensions of contemporary Security: economic, food, technological, environmental, societal, and human. In doing so, it affects the vision of the pragmatic State.

Finally, it is necessary to point out that the National Security approach proposed requires progress towards the achievement of three purposes of strategic scope:

a) The consolidation of the National Security System,

b) The construction of a new National Intelligence System and

c) The development of a culture of National Security following the needs and interests of countries in the 21st century (Gibler, 2010).

National Security policy faces the risks and threats that may compromise the national project and simultaneously identify the windows of opportunity to promote national development and the Security of the State. Institutions performing public functions in Internal Security and Civil Protection are part of a National Security System. National Security will promote the development of capacities to build prospective scenarios and public policy options that will privilege Intelligence over force and the effective coordination of actions in the three levels of government (Gibler, 2010).

- To delimit the areas of competence of the various performers that is part of the System,
- To establish the management criteria and instruments that will make it possible to strengthen the coordinated action of the National Security.

Far from solving problems, any definition is a precarious starting point for reflection. The insistence on an abstract concept and the temporal of National Security, applicable to all contexts and circuits, becomes part of the problem since it tends to separate arbitrarily between the so-called "low" policy the conflicts of opinion and interests of what would be the "high" policy on Security and the problems of force in relations between States (and also in social relations within States).

Generally, this persistence on the absolute concept of National Security tends to "automatically" depoliticize the concept, disavowing itself discussion on the topic. In democratic regimes, it takes an effort to bring the themes of Security, Defence, Intelligence, and Policing to the regular agenda of political issues.

There are, of course, restrictions for especially those related to government secrecy. But there is no reason to think that such purity precludes theoretical or empirical research in this important area of State action (Gibler, 2010).

An important step in advancing the security discussion can be given by evaluating two recent attempts to their perception of the impact of National Security by:

1) The successful attempt to resolve the tension between State Security and Individual Security is strictly juridical and normative.

2) The number of attempts to solve the Moral Intolerant of the concept National Security system through using the concept of human sequence. The criticism of this attempt will have a more accurate assessment of the risks of loss of efficiency in the operation of the Armed Forces and the Intelligence Services, especially in the excessive expansion of the range of defensive requirements and information on the adoption of the concept of Human Security.

The concept of National Interest is pre-democratic; historically, it develops - initially as a public interest, reflecting the early modern separation of the public from the private sphere. Laurens Lustgarten and Ian Leigh 11994: 03-35) recognize that, although in axiomatic terms only the safety of individuals from the Moral point of view, in practical terms most essential and comprehensive single in the conditioning of life of an individual is still his 'belonging' to a State (national citizenship). The insertion of individuals into the family, social class, ethnicity, gender, or age group would not have similar impacts on their security for their existence. Its clear why security involves State are not mere derivations or extensions of the safety of individuals.

6.2. Public International law identifies National Security with State Security

A direct danger is a moment when a public authority gathers, under its control, the methods of power against individual targets or concentrations that the population needs, which must be guaranteed, which do not violate any law.

Coercion is vital for the regular direction of State development in progress in many countries, and even today, when the interests of the State conflict with the interests of any assembly or individuals, the rulers and their administrations have the opportunity to try to coerce, primarily coercive, your will for public purposes, high quality, or public safety.

Despite immediate brutality on a fluctuating scale (from illegal imprisonment, torture, and death of those who disagree with the system to the degree of mass murder of the population), The State is like the people when the system of Insufficient criminal justice and police measures a Self-assertion and illegal actions against people's lives and property may not have potential consequences, or when rulers adopt external protection and protection approaches that significantly increase the gap between the Individual Security and State Security (for example, a model based on atomic prevention, dependent on destruction, ensures that the population is transmitted as a prisoner of equilibrium outside the leading association.

Above all indirectly, the struggle between various assemblies for the control of State assets that allow controlling the population and the region (general conflict, transformation, or any type of "different influence") undermines b the security of the people.

This contradiction between Personal and State Security is an inalienable allusion to a political demand. It manifests itself in a more or less noticeable dependence on the idea of a Political System and the union of each country with the global framework. An assessment in a political debate, how to approach human security refers to issues of legitimacy and difficulties similar to what everyone saw concerning the idea of public security.

First of all, it seems reckless that a favourable status for any connection without something to be thankful for. The excessive implementation of the idea allows the establishment of new guidelines within intergovernmental associations, where the interests of the most prominent section of the nation collide with those of the most vulnerable countries for various reasons. Threats include large complex ofcausal components. The variety of sources and the data were staggering, limitless, and unbiased by the inherent complexity of the hazards. (Kaczorowska-Ireland, 2015).

The challenge is much more significant because of the conflicting collaborations in which the data is available; however, the imbalance and denial of shared data and double-dealing are part of the communication. This makes it challenging to think about sequential actors' security efforts and action cycles. It is to reduce vulnerability and expand public safety limits that there are military, police, and privileged information administrations. Since well-being is dangerous, these solidarity and knowledge associations are also significant in solving the problem. Infrequent characterized by hardships and National Security difficulties.

6.3. Guide to a National Security

It is true that the reference to the Nation potentially also opened up the concept of National Interest to an interpretation in line with Democracy. But the idea of National Interest also included citizens in a (people's) community and thus tended to disenfranchise them again: National Interests became cross-interest, cross-party, and cross-class, rather than through history, culture, and geography, and thus conceived as unchangeable and politically positioned. It was the task of the foreign politician to sound out, formulate and implement them, who then appeared as a statesman in this context or at least wanted to be seen that way.

The reality in a democratic community is banal. The National Interest underlies (foreign) political decision-making processes as an abstract motivation amalgamated from the actions of the political actors involved - an ex-post category. Its definition is incumbent on the government as the elected representative of the democratic sovereign (Kaczorowska-Ireland, 2015). This power of meaning has important political implications and can be abused. This means that the determination of the National Interest is indeed a prerogative of the executive. It is also subject to the checks and balances of the control of power by the other authorities. It must grant them specific opportunities to participate.

Criticism and opposition to the definition of Government by the opposition, media, and academia are legitimate. Still, ultimately they mean nothing more than If we had this power of definition, we would determine the National Interest differently. The evocation of National Interests thus becomes for both sides - government and opposition Increased recourse to ideas under Natural Law is appropriate because the relationship between States is anarchic. Not legality and law, but legitimacy and justifiability come to the fore. Deregulation of international relations achieved. This takes different forms: The deregulation is thus also evident in the devaluation of international organizations that previously organized multilateral collective decision-making processes. Multilateralism "a la carte" is also practiced in alliance policy - as the coalition of the willing. The circumstances under which war can legitimately be waged are expanded: Prevention and pre-emption by military means have been included in the canon of political options. This step finds its analogy in a policy that does not wait and react to emerging geopolitical changes or crises. Instead, it initiates it under the auspices of reshaping the world order (Kaczorowska-Ireland, 2015).

The deregulation of international relations is not an end in itself, but a step and phase on the way to an order adapted to the new risks and dangers. Governments must guarantee Democracy, Human Rights, free-market economies, non-support for terrorism or proliferation. If they do or cannot do it, Regime Change must be forced. The International Organizations must either become instruments for implementing this new world order.

The same applies to International Law. It has to be adapted, or it loses its binding force. The security of citizens and society derives from the right to safety. It is a right for the individual, just like freedom, property, and "resistance to oppression:' Instead of the term safety, we now use the term security.

Homeland security includes:

• Civil Security is provided by three major forces: the national police, the national guard, and the fire-fighters take the preventive and emergency measures necessary for the safety of citizens and their environment.

• Safety in the face of significant risks of natural or technological origin (forest fires, earthquakes, cyclones, pollution, and accidents linked to human activity).

• Contingency plans are set up in disaster emergencies. It aims to mobilize all public and private relief resources, or the White Plan to mobilize health establishments to respond to medical assistance in the event of a major crisis.

Defence is called National Defence because, in its global approach, it does not only concern the armed forces but all administrations concerned with the resources essential to the life of the country. The Sovereign function of the State, National Defence, is one of the components of National Security.

National Defence is based on the following principles:

- Independence (from other States or Alliance)
- Comprehensiveness (civil, economic, military)
- Permanence (works even in peacetime)
- Unit (headed by the executive branch),

6.4. State Secrecy

According to the well-known definition of the sociologist Edward Shils 1996:26), a secret is compulsory retention of knowledge, reinforced by the prospect of punishment in case of revelation. This definition is only in part equivalent to others in the specialized literature, such as that of Sissela Bok (1982:051), who claims to be a secret anything kept intentionally hidden (Mokrosinska, 2020).

Emphasizing this aspect of secrecy as being hidden information Kim Lane Scheppele uses a very concise and comprehensive formulation: "A secret is a piece of information that is intentionally untold by one or more social actors (s) from one or more social actor (s)," .The problem of Scheppele's definition (which is the same as Bok's) is that it is too far-reaching for the discussion to be made about Intelligence and Secrecy. Scheppele recognizes that the intentional retention of information in the relationship between two or more social actors varies according to the contexts of the interaction. Still, its definition does not differentiate between private secrets and public interests. The Shils approach is preferable because it maintains the idea of intentionality and adds an external regulatory element for the retention of information: the punishment legally established in the case of revelation.

Public secrecy is thus distinct from any information that is privately kept secret, which is nothing more than voluntary retention of knowledge reinforced by the indifference of others. In this somewhat paradoxical sense, secrets are a form of public regulation of information flows. There are at least five categories of information regulated by public secrecy:

1) National Defence;
2) Foreign policy;
3) Legal proceedings;
4) Intellectual property and patients;

5) Privacy of citizens.

The public justification for the need for secrecy varies significantly in each category. The first two contain most of the information kept secret based on National Security considerations of the five categories. This is the kind of public secret that will be dealt with in that section of the text. The justification of secrecy based on the potential risk to National Security is not available to private actors but only to the State and its representatives, in particular, situations (Mokrosinska, 2020).

Government secrets are compatible with the principle of transparency of governmental acts only when the justification of their need can be made public. This is what David Luban (1996: 154-198) calls the first-order order and second-order maxims relative to the principle of transparency. A non-aprioristic defence of this concept involves admitting the government's secrecy about norms, procedures, and policies (first-order maxims). The reasons for the secret regulation of such information (maxims of second-order) can be publicly exposed and justified. Nothing prevents the third or fourth order maxima from being adopted by Governments or Intelligence Services to justify a decision to keep specific policies secret. In the case of National Security, there are no ideal antidotes against abusing the use of government secrecy.

At the limit, it must be admitted that this is a kind of effective regulation based on trust (Mokrosinska, 2020). A democratic regime must try to translate the Moral Principle of transparency into propositions of institutional design. Government secrecy maybe compatible with the principle of openness only when decisions about applying this type of regulation to specific information flows are made through publicly established institutional mechanisms in the context of democratic rules of the game. The primary justification for restricting the circulation of information produced or maintained by the Government activities related to National Defence and Foreign Policy is the potential harm that its appropriation by a third party could cause to State Security. For example, weapons systems, contingency plans and mobilization, scientific and technological research of military application, intentions in negotiations of international agreements, the performance of defensive capacities, and other similar things, once known by an adversary or enemy, increase our vulnerabilities and provide a crucial comparative advantage for opponents in conflicting interactions.

In addition to being necessary for purely defensive reasons, the secret is often essential for governments to plan, implement, and complete military and diplomatic missions (Mokrosinska, 2020). A prominent example of the crucial role ofsecrecy is the temptation to surprise in military attacks. Still, one can also argue in the same direction as the success of sensitive diplomatic negotiations (for example, the secret negotiations between China and the United States that preceded Nixon's visit to Beijing in 1972, or the secret talks between Palestinian and Israeli representatives that preceded the so-called Oslo Accords in 1993). In such cases, the justification for secrecy is based on the need to prevent government objectives from being frustrated by the early disclosure of information than on potential National Security damage.

The need for secrecy is also claimed in intergovernmental deliberation processes on the domestic issues considered relevant to National Security (energy, transport, policing, etc.),decision-making processes, the premature disclosure of divergences of opinion within of the Government could be harmful to the safety of operations and the possibility of success of any of the goals and plans eventually chosen. In these cases, the applications of secrecy restrictions are much more problematic in legal and, mainly, political terms from the point of view of democracy (Mokrosinska, 2020).

A final general justification for State Secrecy is the need to protect governing agencies' identities and confidential relationships with specific individuals, groups, and governments. The need for secrecy in these relationships emerges from various contexts and takes diverse forms. However, the most obvious case is the protection of sources and methods in the Intelligence area. In addition to the risk of life for the individuals themselves and their families, the exposure of this type of relationship through the failure of one party to maintain secrecy has chain effects on the future cooperation provision, which is considered to be harmful to the National Security and for the prospect of the realization of governmental interests and policies in the international arena.

Apart from the public justification of their practical necessity and moral validity, State Secrets would not remain secret if they were counted only with the discretion of individuals who share the secretive information or with the indifference of others.

The protection of State Secrets is based on three complementary processes:

1) Classification procedures,

2) Access controls, and

3) Punishments in case of unauthorized disclosure.

In the first case, legally competent authorities identify sensitive information sets to National Security and apply classification rules that define the degree of secrecy required and the intensity of the physical restriction measures for each reporting. Safety classifications are made by assigning external markers that illustrate the importance of each information for National Security (typically, the categories of confidential, secret, and ultra-secret). The attribution of a specific marker for a document or set of information is done - in theory - by a legally authorized official or body (Mokrosinska, 2020).

In the case of information considered highly vital for National Security, for example, the assignment of the top-secret category can only be done by the highest authority in the country or by its express delegation. The secrecy categories also provides access restriction corresponding to the degree of confidentiality assigned; the more secretive information is, the longer it will elapse until it is fully publicized. In the second block of measures (access controls), measures of physical restriction on access to such information imply surveillance, management, storage, and transmission systems, no matter in what specific media the information is.

The security discipline of INFOSEC information systems) is concerned not only with the cryptography of messages and information repositories but increasingly with the reduction of systemic vulnerabilities of production, storage, and communication networks. However, it is essential to ensure that sensitive information of different categories is intercepted by unauthorized users (or by spying) or altered or destroyed (sabotage).

Additional safeguards for the preservation of Government secrets are obtained through access veto systems for unauthorized persons, as well as the avoidance of further restrictions on the circulation of sensitive information through the application of the principle known as "need to know" - "need to-know-only." Veto systems involve applying security screening procedures for all persons applying for employment in government agencies in Defence, Intelligence, and Security.

In areas considered critical to National Security, safety controls are used for both civil and military employees and private companies that maintain contracts with Government agencies (Mokrosinska, 2020).

In the case of Intelligence agencies, in addition to the standardized checks on criminal records and credit and health records, more detailed interviews with relatives, neighbours, and acquaintances about the individual's past are carried out, as well in some countries the application of special tests like the one with "lie detectors" (Polygraph tests). After successfully passing veto and investigation systems to gain access to 'classified' information, public servants must obtain credentials corresponding to the classification level of the information (reserved, confidential, secret, and top-secret).

In general, the level of access depends on the degree of seniority of the official and/or the importance of the position held. It should be noted that, once the access credential has been granted, it does not accompany the official or elected official regardless of the positions he occupies. Periodic security checks are, at least in theory, necessary for the renewal of access credentials.

However, the drastic security procedures for granting credentials are that access to Government secrets also depends on applying the principle of segmentation of the most sensitive information (Mokrosinska, 2020).This principle says that each document or set of information can be accessed only by employees who effectively need to know about their content, not by anyone with an access credential with a consistent classification level. This generates new external markers and additional restrictions for access. In the case of the United States classification system, for example, in addition to the three top security categories, confidential, secret, and top-secret, about fifty additional markers often establish tighter regulation than not having the same legal status the formal system. Based on the "need to know" principle, programs, information, and documents with special access to specific shared information may be selected based on the "need to know" principle. In the third block of measures, if safety procedures fail, the dissuasive elements that differentiate Edward Shils definition of public secrecy administrative and legal penalties come into play. In this case, it is essential to distinguish the obtaining of secrets through the espionage of mere leakage of confidential information to the public (Mokrosinska, 2020).

According to Lustgarten and Leigh 11994: 221-248), because it is a discreet and/or stealthy action, successful espionage opens a breach in the secure information that the Government is slow to realize or even aware of in favour of a foreign Government, regardless of its motivations (ideology, money, blackmail, revenge, etc.), as he cannot claim the Common Good of the Nation he is spying on, nor can he claim the humanity as a whole to justify his action. Whether it is a recruited agent (citizen or permanent resident) or his foreign controller (who may have the diplomatic cover or not), the act of spying is an action that alters the distribution of global power and betrays trust on which citizenship is based.

In a world of States that need to defend themselves, espionage is a criminalized conduct in most legal orders (Tsiarnis, 2018). Even if many spies are not even prosecuted, which is true even for intrinsic reasons the very logic of counterintelligence operations, the point to be highlighted is that the seriousness with which the debate is viewed contrasts with the relative trivialization of the leaks of confidential information in democracies (Tsiamis, 2018).

The cause of this phenomenon lies in the understanding of the jurisprudence that unauthorized disclosure of confidential information is relatively more minor damage than splattering because the publicity of information immediately alerts the Government and triggers countermeasures and attempts to control damages.

It may also be that unauthorized disclosure of classified information has been accidental or that it has been intentionally motivated by the decision to expose some corruption, arbitrary or governmental incompetence that was being concealed through the formal rules of public secrecy. In such cases, even if the agent's motivation making the information public makes a difference for assessing its credibility, the damage to National Security must be contrasted with the eventual public benefit resulting from the transgression.

This is always controversial, and attempts at legal regulation counter its political complexity. In most cases that appear to be in the media, leakage of sensitive information ("leakage is a power resource used by members of the Government itself to launch trial balloons on policies and projects to torpedo a policy they disagree with). In the United States, the inflow of classified information is penalized by administrative measures (from censorship to loss of office or employment), cash fines, and up to ten years imprisonment (Tsiamis,2018).

The importance of leakage of classified information by high-ranking members of the central Government tends to generate, on public discredit for the need to operate classification systems and a defensive reaction from the security organs that can be described such as hyper-classification. Incidentally, failures in any of the three processes explained in the previous paragraphs tend to generate excessive expansion in the other two as a kind of perverse "compensation:' Be that as it may, the central Government is a form of regulation of flows of information widely used in the State with temporary.

Michael Herman 1961 reminds the relationship between Secrecy and Intelligence. Employing information-gathering operations in Intelligence is precisely to obtain information that cannot be obtained (or is difficult to access) through ordinary means. For Kenneth Robertson (1987), Intelligence activity is first and foremost an attempt to discover the secrets of others through the use of mere secrets.

Michael Herman is most cautious in considering that the rationale of Intelligence secrecy rests on three different kinds of consideration regarding: sources, information, operations, methods, and technologies employed.

- In the first place, secrecy is used as a form of regulation when the value of the Intelligence obtained depends on the target not knowing what is known under it. For example, prior knowledge of an enemy's plan for a surprise attack opens the possibility offsetting up an ambush. But this is only possible if the enemy does not know that the victimized attacks will be attacked.
- Secondly, the secret also stems from the precarious legal status of the methods employed to collect Intelligence. Especially in times of peace, espionage, electronic surveillance, and hacking of computer

networks are contrary to the laws of countries/targets and even international laws that guarantee the inviolability of territory, airspace, and territorial waters. The political costs of these violations can be undermined through secrecy, allowing more effective diplomatic management of eventual crises (Tsiamis, 2018).

• In third place, the most substantial reason for the secrecy and vulnerability of the sources to the security countermeasures that the target would take if they knew of the opponent's effort at Intelligence. What is intended to be protected through secrecy is not any detailed information that a source has already provided but rather the continuity of intelligence flows. Secrets profoundly mark the "modus operandi" and organizational culture of the intelligence service, even when the work of analysis is primarily based on ostensible, non-secret sources. It should be noted that there is no direct and univocal relationship between the secret nature of the sources and means of collection and the analyzes produced in Intelligence. There are, however, negative associations between the intensity/quantity of government secrets and the possibility of citizens' control over the government (Tsiamis, 2018).

Therefore, from the point of view of democratic institutional arrangements, applying this type of regulation to a specific information flow would have a double burden of proof: that of the need for secrecy, the effectiveness of the mission, and the guarantee of public control, albeit indirect.

6.5. External Control

Citizens' access to information about what rulers does and what they know is necessary for keeping contemporary governments minimally representative of the governed. One of the main dilemmas faced by democratic theory is reconciling the essential autonomy that rulers prescribe to defend the interests of the governed. The entire functioning mechanisms are capable of ensuring that the actions of the rulers will be conducted respecting the will of the governed. This respect is as much relative to the will expressly be expressed by the governed. It is dose to the later evaluation of the governors' actions by the governed accountability (Gibler, 2010).

This dilemma is complicated when discussing public control over National Security, Government Secrecy, and Intelligence. The tensions between State Security and individual Security, such as the tensions between Government Secrecy and the citizens' right to information, are structurally determined by the anarchic nature of authority in the international system and are more or less acute depending on the nature of the political regimes, forms of Government and other institutional characteristics and political choices of the relevant subjects in each country. Such tensions are unavoidable within the framework of the State system, which represents the modern way of solving the problem of institutional accommodation in complex societies marked by conflicts of interest and opinions (Gibler, 2010).

Concerning the existence and operation of State Intelligence and Security Services, the double tension discussed in the previous sections implies two types of main risks:

1) The risk of Government manipulation of services seeking to maximize power;

2) The risk of self-assessment of the services themselves would be transformed into a kind of parallel power within the State. Generally, in the area of Intelligence and Security, the mechanisms of public control are pretty fragile and uncertain, and the more indirect and horizontal tend to be relatively more effective. This fragility is common. There are needs for training programs and socialization processes for officials of Intelligence. These agencies incorporate high civic values and a high degree of professionalism and respect for the Constitution.

6.6. Intelligence Services

The Intelligence Services are Government agencies in charge of collecting, analyzing, and disseminating information that is considered essential for the decision-making process and the implementation of public policies in the areas of foreign policy, National Defence, and Public Order. These Government agencies are known as Intelligence Services.

Although the use of spies and specialized informants dates back to ancient times in remote areas such as Chennai, the Middle East, and the Roman Empire, Intelligence has acquired a new operational dimension as a social, professional, and permanent occupation of the modern State in Europe. Even then, Intelligence agencies as we know them today only began to institutionalize in the 20th century (Caparini, 2016). After the end of the Cold War, many countries discussed the need and role of these services, which could indicate that their growing institutional weight was only a temporary phenomenon, the product of two world wars and the Cold War itself.

In the first half of the 1990s, Intelligence budgets were significantly reduced, while the new international context became more volatile and, as a result, the demand for information became more and diversified. Be that as it may, as the 21st century dawned and knowledge administrations continued to be a constant element of the State power of nations, the average response to the difficulties of the new global reality as a whole would shift towards a significantly larger number. In terms of more direct competition with other data providers, increasingly scarce assets, and changing global circumstances, the quest for readiness will refer to a technique that relies on three coordinated tomahawks:

1) Speed: assortment, examination, and distribution cycles.

2) Potential: how the great variety of information and innovation in creation has immeasurably surpassed the limit in terms of preparing,

creating, and rebuilding a "collapsed" understanding. Boundary widening here becomes crucial for knowledge associations to make more significant additional contributions to the region's dynamic cycles of Public Safety (Caparini, 2016).

3) Flexibility: As emergencies and foreign policy challenges arise and disappear without sufficient notification, the indisputably requested leadership plan, asset costs, and benefits, invest resources in knowledge partnerships, include an increasing pressure for more visible adaptability, and also a more visible mix of different offices. Although Frederick Martin's Freeman wields several innovative problems and a hierarchical culture for the acceptance of this idea of "skill"in North American think tanks, the problems that arise from the special qualities and activity of knowledge exercises are minimized to a large degree.

This, in general, is a problem little explored by the specialized literature. Acronyms such as CIA, KGB, MOSSAD are relatively familiar to the public, but the average knowledge about their activities and structures is restricted to some picturesque facts or images distorted by the imagination and fictional literature. In this sense, is a persistent trajectory of the Intelligence Services and just their relative opacity, the secret mantle that surrounds their activities? As the transparency of governmental acts and one of the most valued requirements of the political practice contemporary (and the main unfulfilled promise of democracy), it is not surprising that the mere existence of Intelligence Services generates detachment and insecurity in the citizens that question themselves who have such organizations (Caparini,2016).

The negative view that the citizens tend to have of the services of Intelligence of their poses makes transparency a great challenge in the process of the use of these activities. To introduce the theme, let look at the text of Italo Calvino. According to Calvino, visibility as a literary value involves not only the ability to see the reality of the world and tradition, but in originality and invention, the capacity for abstract imagination is absent and decisive and will be negatively affected by the saturation of pre-fabricated images (Caparini, 2016).

This phenomenon would seem to be imperative, which Calvino calls the "pedagogy of imitation:" An education that enables us to express verbally and through writing the polymorphic visions obtained through the eyes and the soul. Although the idea of visibility in Calvino is incomprehensible concerning the idea of three dimensions as a dilemma of nationalization, it is suggestive because it evokes the kind of ambiguity and challenge that must be dealt with in approaching the phenomenon of the transparency of governmental acts. For example, non-transparent visual transparency is used to highlight the invisible ownership of interfaces, which ensures that users can use resources and solve problems without having to go through all the steps and interoperable operations performed by the system. In general, the so-called State activities (where information-gathering activities are included for decision-making) were, in this case, transparent to the citizens, who would look through them to visualize and control the acts of the rulers concerning the ends considered desirable by the political community (Caparini, 2016).

However, bureaucratic inefficiency and corruption make the administrative environment opaque and its governmental acts more conducive to the emergence of a republican principle it's democratically associated with it does not value the invisibility of the system, but rather it seeks the capacity - on the part of the citizen - to visualize and judge for itself what governments are doing in the various spheres of political action. For David Luban (1996: 154-198), the transparency of governmental acts, norms, and policies is a necessary condition for the development of the popular struggle that underpins the democratic institutions and legitimizes the governments' desires to obtain collaboration and obedience from governing. The principle of publicity is a Moral proposition and also a principle of institutional design. No governmental agency or area of Government argues, to remain consistent with the principle of the third party should be built according to operating lines that depend on the secret to its effectiveness and efficiency. However, Intelligence Services are just organizations that depend on secrecy about their methods of inquiry and their sources of information to operate effectively. To the extent that the process of institutionalizing this type of organization implies not only an effort to become stable but also a quest for recognition and value in the eyes of citizens, which depends on transparency. In truth, as David Luban himself says, Government Secrecy and Intelligence activities are compatible with the pre-eminence of the party only when the justification for its existence can be made, itself, in public.

In these terms, Luban's proposal provides an interesting starting point for the analysis of the complexities, tensions, and conditions of possibility associated with transparency as a non-institutional requirement. Although the two normative present themselves as challenges in the trajectory of any organization, rule, or procedure and, in the limit, they constitute a double dilemma of institutionalization.

It is not a matter here of reiterating the technocratic argument about the existence of a trade-off mechanism between agility and transparency, through which gains in one form or another would be at the expense of the other. The authoritarian implications of such an argument are very clear in suggesting, for example, that government efficiency would largely depend on secrecy and bureaucratic insulation. Or, from the angle that institutional gain in this respect necessarily limits the ability of the organizations (Caparini, 2016).

Although it can be argued that legitimacy is one of the conditions that ensure the efficiency and effectiveness(agility) of Government action, it is equally wrong to assume that all problems of agility could be re-established through institutional gains in transparency. "There are several ongoing international research initiatives currently underway, both in the area of intelligence studies of the Intellectual Property

Association (IISAI) and in the field of Intelligence. British SWD Group on Intelligence, the Canadian Association for Security and Intelligence Studies (CASIS), the Consortium for the SWD of Intelligence (Georgetown University), the Harvard's Intelligence and Policy Program (John Kennedy School of Government) History Group (IIHG, headquartered in Germany) to name just a few. In general, we can situate Intelligence studies as a material in the field of Strategic Studies, which can be defined as the field of studies that have the main objective of analyzing the phenomena associated with the use of force to compel.

6.7. Intelligence

It is the activity that aims to obtain, analyze and disseminate Knowledge, inside and outside the national territory, about facts and situations with immediate or potential influence on the decision-making process and governmental action. It's the safeguard and security of society and the State. Therefore, it is understood that the National Defence and the Intelligence Service are closely linked since both aim to protect and safeguard National Interests. The Defence has a more executive role. To make public defence policies are implemented, the Intelligence Activity would have a position to provide the information necessary for the decision-making of the public policymakers (Krahmann, 2010). Intelligence Services have always been present in significant State decisions in the history of mankind.

This activity is closely linked to power relations, influencing events within nations and affecting international relations. Its main objective is to obtain data for knowledge production to assist the decision-making process at different levels. Collected either by an officer on the battlefield or by the planner of public policies.

This activity had its peak in terms of institutionalization, the number of resources available, and importance to the States in the Cold War era. This was the period of most extraordinary commotion for the Intelligence Service, with a tremendous advancement in technologies to collect and analyze information from enemies and allies. Thus Intelligence activity has become a fundamental element in subsidizing the decision-making process of Governments, affecting how States would conduct internal and international relations. At the end of the Cold War, the need for Intelligence Services was questioned, so their budgets were significantly reduced. The response of the Intelligence activity was to adapt to the new budgets and keep information and Knowledge flowing to the rulers.

As the 21st-century approach and new communication technologies, Intelligence Services continued to be part of the State apparatus and are still widely used by rulers today (Krahmann, 2010). The Security Services, Secret Services, and Information Service, called Intelligence Services, comprise the State's organs responsible for collecting and analyzing political, military, and economic information about the other States. These Services also prevent the activity of foreign espionage in national territory, the so-called Counterintelligence, and coordinate the whole set of actions that may weaken the force of Enemy States.

Intelligence activity is not only concerned with information about State enemy. It also works on a wide range of subjects and exemplifies the broad scope of Intelligence activity when it says: The role of Intelligence is the evaluation of Security threats, so Intelligence's area of activity is almost unlimited, both internally and externally. It is necessary to delimit it according to several variables: the perceived threats, the level of existing social cohesion, the degree of international presence sought the resources available to the area, and many others. There is an interdisciplinary in which Intelligence can act. Seeks and analyzes information in any area of society, such as economics, agriculture, and politics. Analysis of others countries, and collect information on any subject that may be a threat or an opportunity for National Interests (Krahmann, 2010). Delineating the area of activity of Intelligence, in addition to using the information needs of public policymakers, there is also the National Intelligence Policy. This division between Intelligence and Counterintelligence aims to meet the routine needs of the decision-making process and follow-up of emergent events and situations, predictable or otherwise, to anticipate both opportunities and possible threats to the Democratic Rule of Law. Such threats are defined as: The possibility of the State losing or being stripped is material possession or political, economic, or military condition.

And Intelligence works precisely with the perception and prevention of these threats. Perception of a threat can be seen as the prediction of some damage caused to the State. It is worthwhile to spend resources on prevention rather than recovering from that damage. Intelligence is one of the components of State Power. So rulers expect it to fulfil its role of maximizing the country's strength in war and peace. Governors need to know about the political nature of the international system, where the profits and gains of one country over the other are decisive for the economic and political survival of the Government and the population.

In the international arena, where the main actors are the sovereign States, the role of Information Services is to optimize resources, so governors understand the situations to take decisions with rationality and clarity (Krahmann,201O). The long-term optimal functioning contributes to making the governmental process more agile informed. The analytical relevance of Intelligence is restricted to issues and problems of National Defence, External Policies, and Public Security to prevent surprises, diplomatic crises, and severe internal threats. The activity is, in this sense, a kind of insurance against a threat that may not be realized but whose potential damage justifies the investment (Krahmann,2010).

Intelligence activity develops within the conjecture of action of a State on strategic issues inherent to its society. Establishing objectives of international position and insertion and defending against possible external threats.

The Intelligence Service proposes to formulate competitive scenarios for the State's participation concerning the foreign market, exposing its values, stability, and position of its sovereignty towards the other nations, which also includes the diplomatic relationship in the presence of international organizations. Intelligence having this enormous task of dealing with information aims at the country's image in the international scenario, the defence of its autonomy for the formulation of its Public Policies, its Sovereignty, and its Diplomatic relations.

And includes in this quota the concern with the competitiveness of its country within the international market, without forgetting its primary function is to maintain a level of security desirable for the nation (Krahmann, 2010).

The international system has gained in complexity because it is constantly changing and because of the high technological advancements in communications. Intelligence Services are being refined to deal with new threats such as terrorism, organized crime, and the proliferation of weapons of mass destruction.

More specifically, Intelligence Services has three main objectives: collecting, analyzing, and disseminating information to help government officials. The collection of Knowledge and Information can be done in various ways: The use of agents who obtain information through other agents is well placed within the governmental apparatus of the target country or organization or as part of the diplomatic corps called HUMINT (Human Intelligence).

There is also SIGINT (Signals intelligence) which is the interpretation, translation, decoding, and analysis of messages intercepted by a third party other than the sender and receiver. IMPRINT (Imagery Intelligence) collects and analyzes photographic images, televised, and other types of visual evidence (Krahmann, 2010). MASINT (Measurement and signature intelligence) deals with measures and signatures. They are part of this area of collection from signals of telemetry of foreign missiles to the monitoring of geophysical phenomena. And last but not least, OSINT (Open sources Intelligence), which is the collection of information from ostensive sources, is the analysis of official documents without security restrictions and the monitoring of the media (radio, television, magazines, and newspapers) on the targets.

The primary function of Intelligence is to obtain information without consent, cooperation, or even Knowledge by the targets of the action. The collection of information can and should also be done in the everyday and leg always of obtaining information, whether by reading newspapers and magazines, requesting information from public documents or even an internet consultation (Krahmann, 2010).

It must be clear here that Intelligence is not only the information itself but also a set of Knowledge about a particular subject. The Intelligence Service collects information, processes, analyzes all raw data, and produces Knowledge that aims to subsidize the decision-making process of the rulers. Among its functions are the support for defensive capabilities planning, military plans and development and/or acquisition of weapons systems, monitoring targets and external environments to reduce uncertainties and increase Knowledge, protect Government secrets, and ensure information and communications Security.

Intelligence, Diplomacy, and the Armed Forces must work together to achieve optimization in maintaining National Defence, goals, and resources (Krahmann, 2010). The Diplomatic area covers the discretion of facts, situations, and scenarios about its host countries. The military area has the function of obtaining and evaluating information about the Armed Forces of the target country or organization and as the diplomatic area-specific information on matters of state interest and adopting protective measures for sensitive and confidential issues (Krahmann, 2010).

Finally, it is necessary to have concise information on what is or is not threats and possible opportunities to keep the country inserted autonomous and competitive in the international scenario. And whoever deals with sensitive information to advice policymakers is the Intelligence Service.

Therefore, a country needs to have an efficient Intelligence Service to make well-structured policies and have a clear, rational, and effective

National Defence policy to protect the interests of the Nation and safeguard the resources and Knowledge of all nationals of a country. Moreover, having information in the current international context is synonymous with having power.

The State is only really established in its sovereignty when it has an efficient and effective Information Service.

6.8. Strategic Knowledge

It is essential to define "Strategic Knowledge" or Sensitive Knowledge since much ofthe work of Intelligence and Defence revolves around safeguarding this Knowledge. According to the strategy can be conceived: As an extended and complex plan that relies on a set of principles of general character and directly operational purposes, closely linked (Grattan, 2011).

Strategic Knowledge is an accumulation of information to give a base to set principles of a general character and have the main goal within State to aid in the decision-making process of the governed. The basis of the formation of Public Defence, Policies, Diplomacy, social policies, investment policies in areas of the nation's development, among others (Grattan, 2011).

Strategic Knowledge, also referred to here as Sensitive Knowledge, is all information generated by the Intelligence System in planning and executing Public Policies. This definition, however, is deficient because Sensitive Knowledge is not restricted only to information produced by the Intelligence Service.

Sensitive Knowledge is all power-generating information coveted by third parties that can impact the security or the State's economy. It requires special protection measures because of their strategic importance for national institutions and the country's development. It is an asset more and more precious because it generates growth, which attracts the attention and interest of other countries (Grattan, 2011). The information collected and analyzed by the Intelligence Service, which is mentioned above, is considered Strategic Knowledge, or Strategic Information.

All the Knowledge is generated by the research of private companies and by the Government. It is also regarded as Sensitive Knowledge for a Nation, the Knowledge of peoples and traditional communities. It frequently demands an awareness of the population and protection against other private institutions, individuals, and even other States. In a globalized world, strategic information is of very high value, and who has access to this kind of information has great power in the hands and a great advantage.

That is why every Nation has its Intelligence Service, to protect the Strategic Information of its country and assure the Sovereign and autonomous Power ofits State (Grattan, 2011). The Intelligence Service that has the attribution of protecting Sensitive Knowledge is an area of Counterintelligence.

1) The counterintelligence area is just a portion of a larger area called INFOSEC - information security.

2) Security countermeasures (SCMs) are measures of protection. The adversary capacities of obtaining information like:

- Programs of classification of governmental secrets,
- Rules of custody and transmission of documents,
- Restrictions to access buildings files to unauthorized persons,
- Use of encryption for the preservation of the security in the communications,
- Awareness programs and education in the area of information protection would be the area that would take care of the protection of Sensitive Knowledge (Grattan, 2011). Counterintelligence identifies Intelligence operations of an adversary detects and neutralizes the intrusive means of obtaining information used by a Government or organization considered hostile.

3) Operations security (OPSEC) is the set of procedures that aim to identify what information about equipment, operations, capabilities, and intentions would be critical for the opponent to obtain. Counterintelligence is an activity necessarily developed by all Intelligence Organizations to identify, prevent, neutralize, or reduce the performance of the Adverse Intelligence Services, it is constantly concerned with the security of Intelligence activities concerning

sensitive government affairs in the fields of National Security and Development (Grattan, 2011).

It seeks to safeguard the Knowledge and/or confidential data derived from the Intelligence System or manipulated by it and the confidential data generated by other national entities, public or private (Grattan, 2011). A country's first line of defences is in the entities responsible for Intelligence and Counterintelligence. These bodies are responsible for the integrity of the intellectual property, national confidentiality, and related interests. Intelligence services collect information and preventive actions to neutralize and frustrate the search for Knowledge of other entities. Counterintelligence work is vital to prevent information that could affect the nation's security or the economy from being used in an erroneous manner, which would be detrimental to the State.

But what can be Strategic Knowledge? What kind of information can become sensitive to a country? All the scientific and technological discoveries are vital for a country and include innovations and research. Strategic Knowledge is all information that can generate possible impact for a nation (Grattan, 2011).

The Strategic Knowledge produced by the Intelligence Services is also about the consistency and logistical organization of the Armed Forces of foreign states, their strategic doctrine, mobilization, employment plans, and weapons in use.

Strategic Information is about military activities and includes patent and secret activities of governments, the content of military alliances, foreign policies, the pace of trade, the activity of political exiles, the conditions of industries, productive and energy resources, and scientific research. Anything that concerns a Nation can turn out to be or become Strategic Knowledge (Grattan, 2011).

Hence the need for a service that can classify and analyze what is or is not Strategic Knowledge for the country. And, given the proper classification, come to protect the Knowledge that should remain within the nation afterall. Controlling and deciding on the functioning of the global socio-economic system implies the use of information; the control of such information automatically confers a position of advantage. It (information) is one of the most critical. The Democratic State of Law demands Security and Information for its decision-making and for its political institutions to persist and fulfil its function efficiently, maintain internal order, and seek to achieve the external interests of the nation (Grattan, 2011).

The current international scenario is highly changing. The State must have the autonomy to generate internal, external, National Defences, and public order policies to be Sovereign. For this reason, he needs to have information on the issues at hand to decide the best possible way to act within the domestic and international context. Intelligence has begun to devote itself more extensively to adversarial relationships, that is, relationships that may jeopardize the security and safeguard of the nation.

As improved technologies have reduced frontiers, intelligence work has become more massive and comprehensive. It has required adaptation to greater agility to match the expectations of the information market. In the 21st Century, Intelligence Service has a much more significant relationship with international relations and competitiveness than in previous periods. The Intelligence activity covers military matters and civilians such as bio-piracy, money laundering, corruption, terrorism in order the State can take political, economic, and diplomatic decisions (Grattan, 2011). Now, these services help to visualize Threats against the Interests of the Country, not to mention the protection of political and economic information, which in the wrong hands can harm a nation.

In addition, in the internal sphere of the Intelligence Activity, information from this service helps to maintain public order and social peace. Counterintelligence has the function of neutralizing the attempt of other countries or companies to acquire Knowledge that may conflict with the National Interest (Grattan, 2011).

Intelligence Activity is part of the standard functions developed by governments, organizations, and companies as an instrument for decision-makers to manage conflicts and overcome obstacles for Government and business actions. In addition, Intelligence identifies threats and may also scrutinize opportunities that will be beneficial to the achievement of the nation's goals and interests. Note that Intelligence has been used for a long time by the States, and we can say that the leading countries of the planet make use of Information Services these days. Even though it sometimes arouses fear and controversy, these services have actively participated in the decision-making spheres of the State (Grattan, 2011).

The main problem is transnational crimes, terrorism, bio-piracy, organized crime, money laundering that require a combination of forces from governments and their respective Intelligence Services (Grattan, 2011). This is the tendency that governments should generally follow. The exchange of information between Intelligence Agencies prevents and combats activities that may cause harm to the security and social stability of a country.

Legislative and governmental bodies have little concern about Defence issues and little Knowledge of the Armed Forces. This creates conflict: on the one hand, the military that has the total weight of the defence of the country in their hands, and on the other side, there is a bottleneck of the Armed Forces by the State structure due to the ignorance of its fundamental purposes, and with this, it drastically restricts the budget (Grattan, 2011).

The lack of interest and knowledge about the work carried out by the Military and the Intelligence agents causes a significant problem in the effectiveness in these. It poses a substantial risk to National Defence. It is essential to break public fears showing a transparent Intelligence Service supervised by the Executive and Legislative branches of the democratic State. Reducing the population's anxiety of having their rights reduced at the time of the military dictatorship and by providing better intelligence activities in the country and thus increasing public confidence in the State Security apparatus (Grattan, 2011).

In addition, the leading nations of the world have an Intelligence Service that, over the centuries, has been assisting its rulers in the central State decisions. The world's major nations have an Intelligence Service that, over the centuries, has been assisting its rulers in the central State decisions. This activity causes controversy and causes fear among citizens, due to the lack of knowledge and anxiety of having their rights and guarantees limited.

It is still very much crucial to explain about the current international scenario, since its main objective is to defend the Nation from transnational crimes such as drug trafficking, terrorism, and trafficking in persons. And for the effective fight against international crimes, it would be necessary uniformity of doctrine in Intelligence. This would help in exchanginginformationbetweenIntelligenceagencies.Suchinternational cooperation is one of the main procedures taken to prevent attacks on the security and stability of countries, making the fight against transnational crimes better and more accessible. Apart from this, no democracy, within the highly changing international conjuncture like the current one, can stop using a legitimate and effective National Defence instrument like the Secret Service (Grattan, 2011).

A country without Intelligence is a country that is constantly surprised, vulnerable, and driven by events like a leaf thrown in the wind. A country without Intelligence will always be a co-protagonist, never a protagonist, in the game of nations. A necessary condition provided by the State to guarantee the prevalence of its territorial Integrity, Independence, Sovereignty, the Rule of Law, political, social, and economic stability, and the achievement of its National Objectives.

The concept of National Security as a function of the State to establish the power of the head of the Executive is to preserve National Security in its respective Law. The concept of National Security is comprehensive. Two postulates converge:

- the first refers to the situation generated by the absence of circumstances that threaten the State within (internal security);
- the second, to how the State establishes a defence system to face these circumstances from abroad (National Defence). National Security is how internal security and National Defence are developed (Grattan, 2011).

The supreme power of the Nation ensures the capacity for free self-determination without accepting any intervention in its internal affairs. It means the supremacy of the legal order of the State in all its territory to face the obstacles that oppose the conquest and maintenance of the National Objectives (Grattan, 2011).

6.9. Antagonisms to National Security

Any type of obstacle and/or interference to National Security, which may be sponsored by another National Power or by non-state agents, or be of natural or anthropogenic origin, prevents or limits National Aspirations, Interests, and Objectives.

They are classified into Risks and Threats.

• Risk Implies a condition, internal or external, generated by political, economic, social, or Non-State agents and disasters of natural or anthropogenic origin, whose evolution could jeopardize national development.

• Threat It is an intentional antagonism generated by another State's power or by non-state agents. Its characteristic is hostile will that endangers a severe violation of National Aspirations, Interests, and Objectives. Threats are classified as traditional and emerging.

• Emerging threats. Those internal or external incidents may temporarily affect the State's security and, at the same time, two or more fields of the National Power.

• Traditional threats. Those sponsored by the National Power of another State endangers territorial integrity, sovereignty, and independence, questioning the existence of the affected country. All are generally manifested by violent actions in the political and military fields.

6.10. National Interests

The needs, the greatest revelation of human dissatisfaction, are first identified in the individual and serve as a reference for groups and the Nation itself. Collective desires, awakened by the needs of the whole Nation, consciously or unconsciously represent the impulse to show the sense of present dignity as a constant in the realization of Man.

To accomplish this when based on values makes the National Community the privileged space of inter-human exchanges that lead to improvement. These desires will boost the service of interests and aspirations.

National Interests are values of internal and external nature. They represent a relationship between the national group and something that it believes indispensable, in time and in asparagus, to define such interest's inappropriate conditions. They are one of the most critical imperatives in the life of any State because they stimulate the Nation to build its future (Gray, 2014).

Alongside National Interests, and at a deeper level, as an accurate integrating dimension emanating from the National Consciousness, are National Aspirations. They become vital since they bind the Nation's survival, identity, and evolution. The ultimate synthesis resulted from meeting these needs, interests, and aspirations and is called Common Good. The Common Ground is translated as a synthesis objective of the National Objectives, when they are more explicit points of reference capable of responding to the Nation's project of its destiny. Government, identify the ways that the governments, acting in the name of the Nation, have the best for the conquest and maintenance of the first (Gray, 2014).

6.11. Intelligence: Operational Dynamics

"Knowledge is concerned with the part of the battle between countries dealing with data."Intelligence seeks to know the world. However, discernment can never forget this embodiment of reality: it involves a struggle with a human adversary who is come on. Reality is not an end but simply a means to win." (Abraham Shulsky, Silent Warfare, 1992, p. 197)

There are two main uses of the term Intelligence outside the scope of the cognitive sciences. A broad definition says Intelligence is all information collected, organized, or analyzed to meet the demands of any decision-maker. Intelligence and a specific layer of aggregation and non-analytical treatment in an informational pyramidal formed based on the vertex's raw data and intuitive knowledge.

The technological sophistication of information systems that support decision-making makes Intelligence designated to this function is it in the government's routine, medium enterprise, or social organizations. In this sense, Intelligence and even knowledge or information is here analyzed. It is undoubtedly possible to theorize about the nature of information and the impact of total flows of data on the economy, the State, and social life in a general way. However, this intelligibility refers to more limited sets of information structured information flows.

A narrow definition states Intelligence as collection of information without consent, cooperation, or even knowledge on the part of the targets of the action. Intelligence is the same as secret or secret information in this restricted sense. Ignoring the narrow definition would imply losing sight of what ultimately makes this inappropriate activity. However, intelligence service activities are broader than espionage in the real world. They are more restricted than providing information in general on any issues relevant to government decision-making.

This poses a very concrete difficulty for a precise action of the activity of Intelligence which pervades it differs from the comprehensive notion of information and the excessively narrow notion of espionage (Caparini, 2016).

Michael Herman separate the collecting and specialized collection system and sources of information (single-sources collection). It follows a stage of analysis of the information obtained from the various single sources and other non-structured flows. The persistent association between Intelligence and conflict is vital, precisely because the two dimmers of the concept are non-dissociable in the praxis of the organizations in charge of providing this type of information and knowledge. The analytical description of the concept analyzes and estimates in Intelligence activities and any other analyses of governmental technical advisory bodies are for intelligence analysis: to increase the awareness of adversaries and to problems affecting national and State security (situational awareness). Intelligence deals with the "other" study. It seeks to elucidate situations where relevant information is potentially manipulated or hidden. An adversary makes an organized effort to misinform, render opaque the understanding, and deny with effect.

The security intelligence services have many purely economic objectives. Still, even these share the condition of others in the eyes of the constitutional party and the constituted political order. The argument applies even to studying facts and problems unrelated to a specific actor. The list of issues on which agencies need to inform their users is growing, ranging from cultural aspects of societies to details of technologies (Wegge, 2017).

New items should be incorporated into intelligence agencies' agenda to "add value “in areas that are not their specialty. But their sources and methods are deemed necessary by civilian and military users. Finally, the more open the sources of information and the less conflicting the issues and situations, the more intelligence analysis will contribute to the mind's decision-making process. This criterion emphasizes the value of a narrow definition of irrelevancy. The frontier of analytical work in Intelligence needs to be broken concerning some connection with the detachment of the analyzed to the governmental decision processes in international politics, National Defence, and provision of public order. Regarding the operative meaning of the concept, the difference between the collection of information for purposes of intelligence production and/ or after government operations involving the systematic collection of information on actors and problems relevant to National Security and more nebulous, impossible to trace, two typical situations in which this difference can be seen are the diplomatic relations between States and military operations (Wegge, 2017).

Usually, countries maintain diplomatic relations. Each Sovereign State allows the formal representations of the other States in their territories to send reports to their governments and nations. Efforts to obtain information through diplomatic channels and intelligence operations are re-evaluated as different by the actors involved, mainly based on the various means used. Diplomats, Military attaches, or international experts suspected of espionage are declared persona non grata, expelled from the country of lodging, and returned to their countries of origin based on the Vienna Diplomatic Relations Conference.

In the case of military operations, it may be more appropriate to speak of a continuum of combat in Intelligence. However, certain specificities have led to Intelligence activity even in combat situations. The most obvious is the degree of control that Intelligence organizations have over each type of information flow. In case of combat information, the data is obtained as a function of the direct contact of troops with the enemy - are used immediately for operational alert or the decision on immediate action (Wegge, 2017).

Data can later be integrated into the information flows that feed into the production and dissemination stage of Intelligence reports are controlled by the functions ofthe command structures of the forces. The Combat Information it's an activity distinct from Intelligence activities. Despite this pragmatic criterion on who controls the collection and the resulting informational flows, it is not always easy to apply the measure. In the Persian Gulf War of 1991, the United Nations military survey was supported by North American satellites and analysts controlled by the CIA and Pentagon intelligence agencies and counting on intelligence operations.

The intelligence work and the battle information management depended heavily on the airborne command and control systems such as the AWACS (Airborne Warning and Control Systems) and JSTARS (Joint Swerve Target Attack Radar Systems) subordinated to the allied command in the theatre. In other words, with greater integration of joint military operations, operational control of specific Intelligence resources and Combat Information can change the sphere of command depending on the needs, as in the case of the army units of tactical Intelligence collection eventually used by the artillery or satellites transmitting signals and/or decoding processed directly on the command of unit commanders in the operating theatre.

Timelines and the growing sophistication of resources available for the generation of combat information (targeting, alerting, and electronic warfare operations) also create new shadow areas between Intelligence and operational information combat, especially between the areas of Intelligence of operations support of electronic warfare. In particular, when it comes to localizing, it identifies and produces countermeasures in the electronic radar and warning systems. It's difficult to know where one thing starts and another. Intelligence cycle

The uncommon descriptions of the intelligence cycle can detect up to ten steps or main steps that characterize the activity, namely:

1) Informational requirements.
2) Planning.
3) Management of the technical means of collection.
4) Collection from singular sources.
5) Processing.
6) Analysis of the information obtained from various sources.
7) Producing reports and studies.
8) Dissemination of products.
9) Consumption by users.
10) Evaluation feedback.

The idea of intelligence culture must be seen as a metaphor. A model that does not correspond to any existing system. On the other hand, this lack of descriptive perception is not what matters since the characterization of activities is Intelligence. At the same time, a complex and directional process of work is essential so that qualitative changes can be distinguished that the information suffers during a cycle of uninterrupted and interrelated work. The main contribution of the idea of the intelligence cycle is precisely to help understand this.

As the activity of Intelligence and itself a subordinate function of the processes of formulas, decision and implementation of Foreign Policy, Defence, and Public Security, we can also think of the cycle of Intelligence as a sub-set of activities of the so-called "public policy cycle": a cycle made by the emergence of problems (issues), the establishment of an agenda, the formation of policies and lines of action, the processes of decision-making, implementation and evaluation.

Information needs, set priorities, and pass them on to Intelligence leaders by the Decision-makers, elected politicians, ministers, senior civilian bureaucrats, military commanders, or police chiefs. They have to identify the gaps. These, in turn, transform those needs perceived by users into information requirements for the responsible sectors through collection and analysis. It is essential to point out this difference between the general planning of information collection and the management of technical means.

Michael Herman (1996: 283-304) and Mark Lowenthal (2000: 40-521) point out in most situations: Policymakers do not have the time or the clarity to specify the kinds of information they need or will need. In these cases, the lists of demands tend to be geriatrics (for example, a request for reports on the "situation" in Colombia), or they are formulated without the Intelligence officers having a precise idea about the purpose of the information in the general context of the challenges faced by the Government (for example, a requirement on the performance of troop transport helicopters of a particular Russian manufacturer, without revealing the area of Intelligence is necessary for decision-making regarding the alternatives of action concerning the conflict in Colombia.)

The uncertain nature of politics and the pressure of patterns of thought derived from experience s more or less recent trends tend to make user "requirements" somewhat more structured than the initial assumption of the model. Formal requirements legitimize and provide authorization for agencies to mobilize their means to produce Intelligence on a particular problem or target. But isn't the only factor determining the intelligence activity cycle. Use a set of organizational and analytical tools to complete detail and address those demands, putting them into more effective informational requirements.

Even taking such risks, Michael Herman (1996: 288) maintains that a proactive role of agencies is preferable and compatible with maintaining a high level of responsiveness. It is accompanied by procedures for the systematic evaluation of users' satisfaction with the intelligence products received and external control mechanisms. According to Lisa Krizan 11999: 13-201, even with the correct use of tools to identify users' needs (e.g., taxonomy of problems, lists of questionnaires, and timing and scope), consider the information flows associated with the requirements present complexity. Analysts call for not only information on the current requirements of users but also a comprehensive range of information needed a broader understanding of targets and problems on which analysts are working.

Finally, it should be noted that collecting agencies also work from opportunities created by eventual security failures of the adversaries. Procedural, cognitive, and even resource scarcities show that the Intelligence activity cycle depends much more on the intelligence agencies' initiative (Wegge, 2017).

Collection and processing the specialized collection activities absorb between 80% of Government investments in the area of Intelligence in the countries. Most of these resources are to the platforms, sensors, and technological systems to collect and process information. The use of satellites in the case of the United States, Russia, China, France, and other few countries that operate such fleets.

The volume of raw data and preliminary information collected is much larger than the reports received by the final users. According to an estimate of the 1980s, only 10% of the information collected would come out of intelligence systems (Wegge, 2017).

The means of collecting and the typical sources of information define disciplines which are specialized in Intelligence, which the international literature refers to employing acronyms derived from the use of the United States in the language for information obtained from human sources, sights for the information obtained from the interception and decoding of communications and electromagnetic signals for the information obtained from the production and interpretation of photographic and multispectral images, measurement and signature intelligence for the information obtained from the onset of other types of emancipation, such as the characteristic and individualized signals of vehicles, platforms, and weapons systems.

HUMINT - the English word for this discipline is typically an American euphemism embedded in international jargon because it avoids espionage. The acronym also indicates that the Intelligence obtained from a human is far from being summarized as archetypes of espionage. The Intelligence officers who work for an intelligence service are accountable for the information-gathering operations and their sources, some of which are agents. The current civil and military HUMINT organizations are responsible for but are also affected by various non-natural sources. Base on the pyramid of HUMINT is the less glamorous source, with access to the less sensitive information and insulating value (Sano, 2015).

Secure services maintain systematic services in ideal interviews; with persons who have access to countries or areas "difficult." Information from travellers and occasional travellers, academic experts, business contacts, or even refugees and individuals from oppressed communities may be helpful. In war situations, an essential source of information is the populations of occupied areas and the prisoners of war POWs interrogated by the Intelligence units of the Armed Forces. Neither of these cases is the source of formal intelligence service. Such programs tend to be conducted by other organization officers, not those responsible for the espionage operations themselves (Sano, 2015).

The degree of clandestine contact with this type of source can vary, ranging from the formal approach to the provision of specific information and the manipulation of sources Obtaining information without the target having conscience about its relationship with an intelligence agency it's a very delicate approach. Agents are aware that spying on their Government or organization provides vital information to National Security for foreign Intelligence services. Volatile agents are viewed with much disagreement by foreign Intelligence services as part of the operations of the Security Services of the target country.

They have as their mission misinforming or infiltrating the Intelligence service that it accepts (Sano, 2015).

On the other hand, excessive suspicion may prevent access to a well-placed source. In the past, the goal by which someone corrodes to spy on an adversary is rather varied and changes over. From the point of view of the Intelligence services responsible for directing the programs and recruiting agents, it is necessary to differentiate two basic categories of Intelligence officers from abroad: those operating with official coverage and the others.

The integration of Intelligence officers into the diplomatic corps of the Embassy or Consulate, disguised as a cultural attaché, political adviser, technician, assistant to the military attaché, representative of the ministry of agriculture, secretary, or any other government official an offense to be in that country, and also to grant diplomatic immunity in case of detection of their own activities, since international law requires that such officers are expelled by the Government (Sano, 2015).

The country's authorities are being spied on and the security provided by the Embassy and Consulates. The intelligence officers can maintain their archives and comprise themselves with the headquarters of their service country of origin. The most senior officer conducting intelligence operations in a foreign country heads the "station" (in the North-American jargon, or the "rezidentura," in the Russian slang) of his intelligence service. Official coverage facilitates the work of counter-espionage surveillance teams of the target population. It limits the types of persons intelligence officers may contact without raising suspicion. In extreme cases where diplomatic relations are interrupted, this deconstructs collecting information. On the other hand, this may limit contact with the official expose the service frameworks to a much higher level, nongovernmental coverage requires a much more extended maturation and training period.

Logistical requirements communications are much more complex. In general, Intelligence obtained from human sources (HUMINT) is not only the oldest and cheapest way of getting secret information, but it is also the most problematic. Management problems range enormous pressure on staff recruited, to the difficulties associated with controlling the credibility of the source and the reliability and accuracy of the information, in addition to the risks. Counter-espionage operations which attempt to neutralize the agents or then corrode them as double agents, a risk is always present in the sources themselves, tempted to fill specific informational data with the information made in paper mills.

In addition to security issues and difficulties in controlling the quality of the information obtained, other operational features of the HUMINT area are derived from the long processes of identification and recruitment of agents, from restricted committees between agents and their controllers, and of all the cognitive and intellectual systems inherent indirect human obeisance. Despite these limitations, it is irreplaceable as a source of information. Especially when it comes to discovering the real intentions of an actor, intercepted messages (SIGINT) or photographs (MINT) are insufficient evidence. Documents and oral explanations present, at least potentially, a degree of comprehensiveness that the other disciplines of the collection have not yet been able to obtain (Sano, 2015).

Spying is often indispensable for effective exploitation of other sources of information like the production of copies of coded books, and ciphered materials have always helped cryptology. Michael Herman (1996:65-66) says there is a tendency for organizations specialized in HUMINT to function as multi-purpose organizations, developing new forms of collection of data through technical ways.

SIGINT - the second ancient discipline of collecting information is the Intelligence of sin or SIGINT (signals intelligence). Historically, SIGINT has originated from interception, decoding, translation, and analysis of samples by a third party, besides the issuer and the intended offender. Deciphering and/or decoding of intercepted messages Intelligence is divided into two compliant fields, called COMINT (communications intelligence) and ELINT (electronics intelligence). The Intelligence of communications is obtained through the interception, processing, and pre-analysis of the communications of governments, organizations, and individuals, except for the monitoring of public radio and television broadcasting, which fall in the onsite area. The access to transmitted messages, one can also monitor the traffic patterns of messages between different points (traffic analysis and direction); traffic and localization of transmissions are an integral part of the COMINT discipline (Weinbaum, 2017).

In turn, electronic Intelligence, or ELINT and obtained through the interception, processing, and pre-analysis of non-communicative electromagnetic signals emitted with civilian equipment, except for the reissues resulting from nuclear explosions, which fall in the area of the primary specialization. The first targets of the ELINT operations were the radars of the air defence systems. With the development of the missiles and the proliferation of the use of electronic equipment throughout the Cold War, they will have other priority targets for various types of radar, mainly operating systems (target acquisition, browsers, mobile phones, etc.) and command, control, communication, and intelligence systems.

According to Jeffrey Richelson (1999: 182-1851),the ease with which exchanges, as well as electronic signals, can be detected and decrypted depends on the transmission strategy of the frequencies used and the use of security strategies, particularly encryption. The most reliable method of sending meaningful, non-transferable data, but "quiet radio" and emission reduction programs are at odds with the need to match overwhelming associations and human frustrations, or less inevitable (Weinbaum, 2017).

Throughout the INTELSAT International Telecommunications Satellite Organization satellites network, more than two-thirds of all international telephone traffic passes, virtually all international trunks of television signals, as well as most digitized fingers and - mail, video, and teleconferences. Given the disparity of media in the area of intelligence gathering, the capacity such as the United States and, to a lesser extent, the other Western European countries of NATO, Russia, and China, tends to be much higher than the capacity of other governments or companies guarantee the safety of their Icomsecj commissions, even with the cheapening of new ITIC information and communication technologies.

European Parliament investigations in 1999 on the so-called Echelon, only the United States network of ten fixed stations monitoring global satellite communications intercepted a monthly volume about the number of messages, including the Internet, telephony, cell telephony, bank transfers, fax services, and other signals.

Considering all other systems and platforms combined the interception capacity of the United States and much more significant than that. According to Matthew Aid (2000: 17-21), as early as 1995, the central agency of the US INS) was able to intercept a volume of signals of 1quadrillion bits every three hours of operation of platforms and sensors in the whole world. The major problem of the SIGINT area would be the lack of ability to process such vast volumes of intercepts.

Current estimates for the United States and China point to re-examining one input system for each reporting. And the processing of the volume of intercepted traffic is no less necessary than the low yield of helpful material in re-reading the total volume. While the NSA was able to process 20percent of everything intercepted in the 1980s, since the explosion of new technologies in 1990, the agency would not process more than 1% of all intercepted material. Processing, decoding, translation, storage, retrieval, and dissemination of systems are as necessary as or more decisive for investment in research and development, such as technologies, sensors, and collection platforms (Weinbaum, 2017). Especially in the North American, Chinese and Russian cases, in addition to sizeable terrestrial traffic interception stations, listening posts are also used in foreign capitals (for interception of official short-distance communications, including cellular phones), operation centres, and from mobile aircraft and drones (UAVs) to ships and submarines equipped with sensors and personnel specialized in the collection of signs.

Since the 1960s no platform has been so important like satellites of electronic surveillance and interception of communications. These large "ears" or "aspirators" began to be placed in space orbit even before the imaging satellites and constitute the majority of spy satellites basically. They existed currently main types of satellites of SIGINT.

IMPRINT - it is a specialized discipline of information gathering and subsequent use of the military aircraft for reconnaissance and surveillance. During and after the two wars of the 20th century, photographic images, televised images and other types of visual evidence are also obtained by intelligence officers, reconnaissance patrols, and surveillance teams on land and at sea. However, the development of the mind as a specialized discipline for collecting information was mainly based on photographic cameras and aerial-space platforms (Weinbaum, 2017).

According to William adorn (19 97: 791) and Jeffrey Richelson (1501), the historical roots of collection and use of visual evidence for the production of Intelligence go back to the drawings made by military officers in reconnaissance missions, terrain, panoramas, fortifications, ports, etc. have historically been part of the necessities for the planning and execution of military operations. However, current aerospace platforms for collecting visual evidence have had recent ROMs in the company of aerostiers (balloons) organized by the French after revolution of 1789 or in similar attempts to use balloons for reconnaissance missions by troops of the United States during the American Civil War of 1861-1865, and later in the late 19th century by the British and German armies.

Ever-changing chambers, films, and lenses for vertical and oblique photos, mounted on aircraft and adapted bombers, an intense and systematic exploration of visual evidence in the production of in - of the Cold War after 1945.The nature of the territory of the Soviet Union and the lack of access to other sources of information led the United States to intensify high-altitude aerial photographs over Soviet territory.

The United States used several aircraft types for reconnaissance missions over the Soviet territory; U-2s, high-speed, range, and altitude were unreachable by Soviet interceptors. The episode of the overthrow of one of them by Soviet planes in 1960 was the milestone of a new stage in developing the area of IMPRINT (Weinbaum, 2017). The United States, and soon afterward the Soviet Union, succeeded for the first time in orbiting spy satellites capable of flying over hostile territories and photographing targets on an impermissible scale with the systems then available.

With much more limited resources than those available to the United States and Russia, these countries include (or will consist of in the following years) France, China, India, China, Israel, South Africa, Canada, North Korea, and Taiwan. Over the last decade, technical and political advantages of satellites as far as they are concerned in which commercially sold images with better resolution. In general, these developments have contributed to the discipline of mind every time central to the operational dynamics of the collection activities of Intelligence. In the first place, image satellites can cross the territory of a country without being considered by international law as a violation of the national airspeed. Image satellites moves in relatively low altitude circular orbits than SIGINT satellites.

The North American imaging satellites known as KH-ll advanced operate with 241knI of perigee and 965knI of apogee. Orbits, the altitude, and defined according to the needs of greater accuracy of the images collected, or with greater amplitude of area to be coherent in each periodical passage in the same areas of interest to the Earth's orbital plane. One can rotate the orbital gradually along the annulus to compensate for the passage of Earth around the sun. This ensures that the photographic images will always be in the same conditions of sunlight.

In addition to the work of photogrammetric and interpretation, the successive generations of satellite images were improved concerning the permanence period in orbit, for the adjustment of orbital parameters, to data transfer systems and concerning payload. While the first satellites recover their images in films that, once exposed, were ejected and needed to be collected after their re-entry into the atmosphere with the use of digital systems since the 1980s, photographs and other digital images are automatically transmitted to the station to ground directly. This has led to an increase in the useful life of the satellites and greater agility in the collection and processing cycle.

MAINT - known as intelligence derived from generalizing in the United States since 1986, as an attempt to classify and agitate an array of activities, programs, and specialized agencies that are not easily accommodated in the most established collection practices of visual or communicative pieces of evidence from the use of the media. The unification of this set of activities under the same rubric was due more to an organizational need than to some common trace between phenomena observed or even among the technical merits used for monitoring (Aid, 2013).

In the North American context, they are part of the main area from the collection and technical processing of hyper spectral and multispectral images to the interception of telemetry signals from foreign missiles being tested, including the monitoring of geophysical phenomena (acoustic, seismic, and magnetic by the measurement of levels of nuclear radiation in the earth's surface and in space by recording and analyzing unintentional radiation from electronic equipment and radars and to stay here, by collecting and analyzing physic-chemical materials (effluents, particles, waste, parts of foreign equipment, etc.). According to Jeffrey Richelson 11999: 214-2401, at least three types of North American satellites carry dedicated sensors for the collection of masts:

1) The satellites of the DefInP Program lDSPI are equipped with infrared sensors (different from the sensors used for the production the data derived from these sensors allow the identification of the types of buses used and the spectral signatures associated with different systems of missiles. In theory, any terrestrial events that generate enough radioactivity infrared sensors to be detected from space can be measured and identified by the DSP satellite sensors)

2) NAVSTAR Global Positioning System (GPS) satellites are equipped with nuclear INUDETj. Although the primary mission of NAVSTAR satellites is to provide accurate location data for target acquisition and navigation purposes, the orbit of the 17,700-kilometer orbit of the constellation of 21 NAVSTAR satellites has made the Pentagon also used for the global monitoring of nuclear detonations, which can be detected by x-ray, gamma and pulse electromagnetic.

3) The satellites IDMSPj are equipped with sensors for electromagnetic radiation and "tracking" of pieces of nuclear explosions in the atmosphere. In addition to sensors installed in spacecraft, other technical means used by the United States for collecting masts involve airborne platforms for detecting and collecting samples of chemical and bacteriological agents in the atmosphere, fixed straps for monitoring missiles [such as the station radar "phased COBRA DANE, located on Shemya Island, Alaska], seismological laboratories at Air Force technical intelligence centre, passive radars boarded on

warships, for monitoring of re-entry space vehicles, undersea hydrophone networks for acoustic monitoring submarines, and spacecraft over the ocean (Aid,2013).

One of the main functions of the main area and the collection of information on singular characteristics - the signatures - of weapon systems, combat vehicles, aircraft, ships, and radars for the assembly of databases and later employment in systems of acquisition of target, or for the production of military intelligence and monitoring of international treaties, especially in the nuclear area.

OSINT - the proliferation of electronic databases available on the Internet has greatly expanded the work of collecting understandable data from very specific and obvious sources. A generous understanding of the obvious sources, or OSINT, is invariably central to any legislative knowledge base, yet there is a reasonable written agreement that its meaning has been filled in lately regarding the supposed "educational explosion" of intelligence.

Generally, it includes the legal publication of official reports on the scale of the activities and military power of the United States, without security restrictions, immediate and unclassified perception of political perspectives. The military and monetary components of the internal existence of various nations are focused on monitoring the media, radio, and broadcasting, the legal recording of certain books and diaries of a common and logical person, in a fairly wide range of available and permitted sources under the strictest security restrictions (Schaurer, 2013).

When open political regimes and strict measures of security of a target for the circulation of information, plus the amount of intelligence potentially obtained from political programs, under the most restrictive conditions, the volume of available ostensible information tends to be very high.

For example, it is now known that during the Cold War, a joint program of the CIA and the u.s. Air Force summarized and/or fully translated most of the techno-scientific publications of the Soviet Union. As early as 1956, $ 50 meant the actual content of 328 scientific journals and about 3,000 books and monographs per year. With the end of the Cold War, the acceleration of globalization, and the advent of new information and communication technologies, the availability of ostensible sources increased enormously (Schaurer, 2013).

According to the Deputy Director of Central Intelligence, in 1992, the CIA foreign media watch service (Foreign Broadcast Information Service – FBISI) monitored 790 hours of TV programming per week in 50 countries and 29 different languages. The FBIS monitoring events were then located in places as different as Abidjan, Aran, Asuncion, Bangkok, Panama City, Hong Kong, Islamabad, Key West, London, Mbabane, Nicosia, Okinawa, Seoul, Tel Aviv, and Sierra. Of techno-scientific publications and conventional media, in 1997, the CIA and OIA OSINT programs already had commercial access to nearly eight thousand databases of electronic data via the Internet, in addition to the signing of two thousand electronic journals. In the case of the United States, the main programs and offices available for the collection of ostensible information are the agencies and departments in charge of the analysis stage in the intelligence cycle (Schaurer, 2013).

6.12. Information Security and Counterintelligence

The most elementary operational dynamics of the area of ineligibility are also less understood by outside observers, and the one engendered from its conflict with the security measures that are taken by a potential target to protect its information. Starting from the restrictive practice of intelligence running the risk of exaggerated formalization-while intelligence seeks to conquer what the co-managers and rulers who direct it need to know about the problems and problems related to the identity of the State and the citizens, the area of Information Security, seeks to protect the information that, once obtained by an army or an enemy - for example, after the intelligence operations of a foreign government could make the State and the citizens clear and unstable.

The area of intelligence and the area of security exert symmetrical and mutually dependent factors. From the operational point of view, while the main task of the lobby area is to try to find the "or," the main part of the area of information and ensure that the "others" know what they know about us. The two objectives are fulfilled in the contemporary State by distinct organizations, and Security can be considered as a managerial function in organizations and a responsibility of the command in military organizations.

But psychosis occurs because both activities exist simultaneously and interact in a more or less synergistic fashion for each actor involved in an informational conflict. On the other hand, the dialectic between Intelligence and Security is more complex than the mere offensive dichotomy. The first component is formed by the protective measures that "mirror" the adverse capacities of obtaining information.

Such measures range from programs for the classification of government secrets, special storage, rules of custody and transfer of documents, physical restrictions on access to prisons and archives for unauthorized persons, investigations of personnel employed before the granting of credentials of access to the classified information and surveillance of their contacts with foreign and foreign personnel, the various policies and layers of electronic security in computer networks and the use of cryptography for the preservation of the segregation of communications (COMSEC).

In the military area, this set of ISCM countermeasures, or seizures, also includes the use of muffling to evade the signals of imminent enemy forces, reductions in intentional signatures "as measures against MASINT, training to withstand interrogatories, and other preventive measures against the collection of HUMINT.

Educational programs in the area of protection of knowledge fall into this first "family" of actions in the field of knowledge the second set of measures of intelligence depends on the identification of intelligence operations of an adversary, the detection and neutralization of the intrusive means of obtaining information used by a government or organization considered hostile (Schaurer, 2013).

As Michael Herman (1996: 168) wrote, an agent may be arrested, a foreign intelligence officer acting under diplomatic cover may be expelled from the country after being declared persona non grata, but also microphones and telephonic tapping maybe " and can be felled or forced to save, collection races of squint can be captured in case of breach of territorial waters, and so on.

For all these measures, knowledge accumulated by the counterintelligence area is fundamental. Thirdly, due to the safety of the operations hereinafter referred to as the set of procedures aimed at identifying which information on equipment, operations, capabilities, and intentions would be critical for an individual to obtain (Schaurer, 2013). However, this analysis proposes a set of measures to actively deny such information to the Adviser. Although it also involves some programs for the reduction of noise and unintended signals, radio alerts, camouflage, and others, which could confuse this area of operational security, stands out fundamentally for its active dimension, especially what military literature calls deception operations, used to mislead and induce an enemy to error through the use of accomplishment, deceit, concealment, and dissimulation, causing it to produce a misleading analysis of the situation.

6.13. Covered Operations

These called covert operations are named differently and cover varied activities in different countries but have been widely used by major international potentials throughout the 20th century, which is even more controversial than conventional intelligence operations. In the United States, these are called covert actions (CAs or covert Actions), and, in England, by the simple name of special political actions (SPA). Although it is not possible to develop here a complete analysis of the problems associated with this type of activity, at least one of these aspects deserves a summary. The first aspect relates to the types of operations encompassed by the concept, while the second aspect relates to the relationship between such covert operations and the collection activities analysis and counter-intelligence discussed here (Schaurer, 2013).

Covered events are used by a Government or organization to attempt to systematically influence the behaviour of another Government or organization through the manipulation of economic, social, and political aspects relevant to that actor, in a manner conducive to the interests and values of the organization or Government it sponsors the operation.

According to Mark Lowenthal (2000: II-113) and Abram Shulski (1992: 83-85), the two main attributes of covert problems in the use of force are their instrumental face to implement strategy and the need for persuasion to deny the power. The main component is that clandestine tasks serve as a means of coercion in the execution of external agreements, such as, for example, monetary prohibitions or the scope of choice, identified with the use or danger of the use of Power. The subsequent person emphasizes the rejection of initiation rather than the centrality of the actual activity. Secret tasks can be grouped according to the Scale and Power of the intended use of force and the level of probability of denying creation (McElreath, 2021).

Four types of covert operations can be selected:

• The first type and the most extraneous, involving the membership of existing groups for financing and organizing groups for the war and underground warfare, paramilitary operations, guerrilla warfare, counter-terrorism, or terrorism campaigns. The involvement of a government in such cases can range from financial support and the provision of weapons, explosives, and equipment, to a more direct engagement in logistics, training, intelligence, and combat fighters specializing in special operations Historical examples of such operations include, among many others, the "secret" war conducted by the United States in Laos 1960-1975and the British counter-insurgency campaign in Malaya 1950.

• The second set of covert operations involves so-called "wet affairs," ranging from support for coups d'état and attempted assassinations of leaders of the government forces, including irregular military operations at a border, sabotage, and perpetration of acts terrorists. Examples of such operations are the CIA-sponsored coups in Iran (1953) and Guatemala 1954, the American campaign of destabilization of the Allende Government in Chile (1970-1973), the assassination of Palestinian leadership in the 1980s, or the sinking of Green peace's Rainbow Wanior by the French secret services in 1985 and the 2011 Operation Neptune Spear, of May 2, in Pakistan to kill Bin Laden.

• The third type involves operations of economic and political sabotage against opposing forces or, on the other hand, Governments and allied forces, such as political parties, neo-governmental organizations, communication means, etc. The training of the security forces and intelligence of the post-revolutionary regimes of Yemen in the 1970s by the East German foreign intelligence service, or the help of the Soviet Union's Communist Party to about parties and groups in foreign countries until the 1980s.

• The fourth type of covert operations comprises a set of measures to try to influence the perceptions of a Government or even of society as a whole, through agents of influence, disinformation, and falsification of money or documents, in addition to the various types or types of transactions. This is the type of covert operation, and there are examples; perhaps the most fertile ones were the Free Europe and Liberty radios, clandestinely established by the CIA in Europe in 1949 and 1951.

7. Building an Information System

Data sciences a discipline that examines the properties and behaviour of data, the powers that control the flow, and the resources required to work with data to ensure maximum availability and usability. It includes a piece of genuine scientific research that is not related to its application and a piece of applied science that creates elements and controls (McElreath, 2021).

Data Management (IM) helps increase the intensity of authoritative and business modernization cycles in line with the insight into key data preparation and use and related advancements, as well as data quality details, the content, and the security of the data in the company. Is the utilization of capacity and the retrieval and distribution of data to information banks and PC organizations suitable for a variety of environments. Data society a combination of people who, with mechanical changes, had their parts of durability and improvement, based on the creation, accumulation, transfer, and extreme use of information resources. Each structure, whether it uses or does not have information technology assets, controls, and data production, can generally be considered an information system (McElreath, 2021).

7.1. Information Technology

The term "Data Technology" means any type of activity, including data processing and correspondence through integrated electronic equipment. The term is broader and refers to "a wide range of innovations that work with data, such as the ordering of data, the computerization of the modern cycle, the correspondence between two PC associations or the individual use of computing resources refers to the assets used by the company to prepare and process information. These assets include teams, programming, exchanges (voice, information, and video), and related workforce. Data innovation is the possibilities presented by PC applications - programming and media communication. Improvements and applications that combine the preparation and accumulation of information with the limitation of the transmission range of broadcast communication. It is the fundamental part of information processing, as well as data and correspondence through coordinated electronic teams (Reuter, 2019).

Innovation is characterized as the systematization of information, especially logical and exclusive, which is applied to a certain part of the action; it can also be considered as a science consistent with a strategy. Innovation is a collection of coordinated data in different ways(logical, observational...), from different sources (logical discoveries, licenses, books, manuals, drawings...) obtained through different strategies (research, improvement, duplication, understanding...) and is used in the creation of labour and products.

The creator adds the information and capabilities used to create mechanical links are innovative capabilities. The evolution and coordination of IT components (hardware, programming, correspondence management, workstations [CAD, CAM, CIM, etc.], robotics, and smart chips) have altered lifestyle choices to broadcast, think and work together. As data innovation is integrated into the creation framework, it will radically change the design and way of doing work, especially in the creation and coordination of types of information technology. To get help on the potential for a key use of IT, it is important to know how it works. It may well be considered as auxiliary classifications:

a) Technology, equipment;

b) Informational framework;

c) Automation of workplaces;

d) Development and plan for PC

e) Industrial computerization;

f) Specific components of robotization;

g) Multimedia resources. The systematization of the most important device of information technology is a summary of the guidelines for research applications of the fundamental methodology and it must be constantly updated as any order in the field of information technology is rapidly becoming obsolete. Due to the speed of advance in this area, IT instances:

a) Technologies for the organization of innovative data: information technology, visualization, and information cycles, procedures for planning an information technology master plan;

b) Frame promotion technologies: procedures for creating frames, approaches, project managers, software testing and problem-solving strategies, methods, frame research, specialized frame plan, strategies, models, specialized site information plans, methods, programming;

c) Programming assistive technologies: frameworks, board dataset; programming processing, utilities, screen execution, programming language, fast execution;

d) Technologies for creating cycles and tasks: TFp, volume organization, execution by performers;

e) Hardware support technologies: supercomputers, huge evaluation PCs, PC organizations, nearby organizations connecting miniature centralized servers, microcomputers, RISC engineering, and realistic stations. With information on the different types of IT out there, the next step is to see how they can be used in partnerships to help authoritative methodologies.

7.2. The use of Information Technology in Organizations

The rapid changes in the business climate suggest that associations will adapt and seek more effective approaches to fight and break away from the opposition. Data technology is also the centre of a significant number of developments used by associations to succeed or even continue.

Data transmission technologies are currently used as a means of increasing seriousness, winning, and maintaining an advantage over rivals. This expanded key use ofIT has to do with adjusting the creation of data work in associations. Until the 1960s, data used to be associated with manufacturer management customization, creation, and distribution (Yang, 2020).

The main data frame was created as a start-up framework called Electronic Accounting Machines (EAM). The Management Information Systems (MIS) were created to offer to expedite the required announcement. Around that time, the use of IT meant the computerization of monotonous tasks, and the options of interest in IT were generally evaluated in terms of cost reduction and accelerated a dynamic course of explicit leaders and leaders on a wide range of topics.

The minicomputer also helps the use of IT in companies that did not have the financial capacity to put resources in a centralized server; the benefit of the interest in IT is associated with a decrease in costs. Personal computers and exchangers, equipment, and personnel are associated with the preparation of basic information. Customers gain access to information online by consulting at the workplace or by submitting reports.

The server farm is also responsible for promoting various programs that are prepared and updated for clients. Likewise, it was normal to have a Management Information System (MIS) unit. During the

1980s, the idea of data should be an important asset, a potential source of advantage, and an important weapon. The underlying structures seemed to guarantee the strength and prosperity of the organization.

Later, information technology became more ubiquitous, with business execution increasingly dependent on its application. The presentation (PC) and expansion of hardware and programming standards have caused the adjustment of associations and the pretence of IT. Since a PC was less expensive than a centralized computer, administrators began to encourage individual applications beyond the control of the MIS unit, leading to the decentralization of data.

These applications would meet the needs of the department. Information technology has involved all the important parts of the organization, many internal developers, experts, and many computers (or remote computers connected by media communication organizations) and possibly many end customers in a partnership who have used similar information to various applications. Information, rather than being limited and restricted by basic information processing, was used by many representatives of their PCs, each more impressive than huge PCs for much of the 1980s.

This structure introduces administrative and institutional changes, and the new hardware makes the product even more wonderful and easier to use for new users. In a couple of hours, workers can learn that they are not ready to use a word processor and plan plans and the use of broadcast communications on a microcomputer. Plus, you can now plan your simple frameworks and applications for end customers without the help of software engineers.

By the mid-1990s, information technology was transforming business significantly. The development of innovative activity is associated with the logical and mechanical advance in the field of innovation in the field of data, the tension of an undeniably aggressive climate, and changes in working procedures with companies. Among business systems, jobs, and technologies, on the one hand, there is a growing dependence on programming, hardware, information, and broadcast communications, on the other. Adjusting any of these parts often requires changes to different parts.

The mechanical development of microcomputers, the development of correspondences that transmit information, voice, sounds, and images, the use of PC and broadcast communications for the further development of elements, management, and associations, to distinguish more and more accurately the profile of the information society. Today, information technology is helping to create and disseminate information and data throughout the association through new information frameworks and applications, providing access to information throughout the organization and organizations by correspondence.

IT is now seen as a critical device for starting a business, and its use is becoming the focal point responsible for reaching partnerships, regardless of whether the degree of resistance becomes more visible in intensity (Reuter, 2019).

The dependence of institutions on information technology is evolving. Considering its importance for development, as well as its enormous work to increase the intensity of the institution, the organization of its use should be essential for hierarchical methods.

The methodology for using an IT association must be consistent with business procedures. Such a procedure should guarantee the allocation of some of the assets for IT projects and give rules for their organization and needs. However, what we have found throughout history makes it difficult to find such a propensity. Critical components that exacerbate the mismatch between business systems and IT systems like:

- Pressure from providers of innovative business solutions;
- The IT model of the dashboard is linked to the generally accepted models of pooled data;
- The profile of your expert management;

- IT specialists with a dream are too specialized;
- IT vision and business goals rather than implications;
- Don't think about IT in a meaningful environment;
- Discrepancies in the training of the Chief Information Officer (CIO) and the Chief Executive Officer (CEO);
- Distribution of drawings for the end customer;
- Unkempt promises;
- Disputes over space and power;
- Internal association;
- Lack of scattered commitments to achieve/ dissatisfy improvement in IT activities;
- Low interaction of the CEO with his space;
- Incoherence between the management of the IT society and the IT council of their business areas;
- Correspondence problems by language;
- Decrease in its collection;
- Low responsibility of top management in the achievement/ disappointment of organized IT events;
- The position of the CEO in terms of his legal capacity;
- Lack of prioritization of activities by IT specialists;
- Low level of understanding of the systems;
- Problems during the elaboration of procedures;
- High staff turnover in the CIO workplace;

Recognized evidence of the use of Information Technology on the side of authoritative methodologies can, and often does, through almost natural interactions. However, there must be a systematization of this entire cycle. To work with the most common way of using IT as an important asset, several fundamentals must be learned: ideal elements and ideas of interaction, the execution of vision and vision structures, vital to explore problems/structures and find creative approaches.

The measures that information technology can use to make the organization more aggressive, which are key parts of the business system, can help understand the search for answers to a vital effect. By thinking about these issues, managers could better assess whether their companies are willing to use IT as a tool for authoritative methodologies. The value of the odds and benefits of using data innovation must be consistent with the accompanying advancements:

- Understanding of the ideas of the main powers and methodologies;
- Defining the serious powers that underlie the organization;
- Defining the procedures that the organization undertakes;
- Evaluation of the impact of information technology;
- Determination of the level of trust in the organization's information technology;
- Definition of fundamental freedoms for information technologies.

Strategic impacts that IT can create, thus summarized:

a) Causes changes in work cycle associations (work turns out to be more unique, decreases in existence, and gives consistent information on the best approaches to work with the company)

b) Provides coherence between different specialized units of the association level and beyond its limits (virtual chain of creation). Business intensity depends on reliable communication with suppliers and customers, which can also be established through IT;

c) Changes the serious perception of multiple companies (vital collusions and beneficial agreements between bidders in which organizations participate to exchange assets and administrations, obtaining an advantage);

d) Provides new fundamental freedoms to associations, causing an assessment and redefinition of mission, goals, methods, and objectives;

e) Demand changes in the methods of administration and creation of the authority, anticipating changes in the hierarchical culture.

The implementation of mechanical developments often requires socially specialized changes that require a long period to adapt. This goal is not difficult to achieve in light of people who are opposed to change, such as those forced to join an association, relative to what representatives face when their work is updated.

This is a major obstacle to life change. Therefore, for this cycle to be effective, IT implementers must have a more visible understanding of authoritarian change the level of complexity of information technology management.

The exams in this space can allow members to act and understand the cycles of definition and implementation of approaches to the use of data by an innovative organization to solve the problems of the State, identified with the standards of Morality, Values, Civil Society, Rights and Reliability - The included experts will be ready to:

- Know the possibilities of data innovation in solving problems of leaders of State institutions.
- Structured data.
- Define a framework for data innovation.
- Selection and evaluation of specialized organizations in the field of data management and innovation. A specialized profile of those included will be produced after the opportunity to progress by bike. With the etymological term "innovation;' problems arises for creating a complete separation between the terms "data;' "data structure," and "innovation." Running IT requires a comprehensive update of capacity data, which is highly dependent on human resources, especially given the margins between workforce relationships, capacity for change, and ingenuity.

7.3. Security and Information

By stating that a society must have certain facilities or administrative units, a government agency publishes a public that is organized to work in a particular industry, such as training, welfare, security, and government assistance. IT presents it as an essential part of the preparation of information, as well as data and correspondence through embedded electronic equipment. Therefore, directly supply items or administrations to those who paid for them by collecting fees (Yang, 2020). Data is information (written) in composite (printed or expanded), oral, or modified form. The data includes the bearing component. This is the path to the soul, sent through a message recorded in a space-time medium.

The data can be characterized as reality, reason, and statement. The term data has credits attached:

- Equivalent word of reality,
- The power of the known at the moment,
- Freedom to choose your message,
- The raw material from which the information is extracted, that which is traded with the rest of the world, is more than simply acquired in an inactive state, is characterized by its consequences for the collector, which reduces vulnerability in the given circumstances. Data and information are linked but not interchangeable. It is also important to recognize two types of information.

There are:

- Implicit information. Is it reasonable information about the aggregate of a given topic, which includes feelings, beliefs, moods, and various components, identified with the experience and character of the person who possesses this information;
- Explicit information. Is the data set based on someplace, such as media (books, archives, etc.), that describes the information available on a specific topic;
- Strategic knowledge. It is the mixture of unequivocal information and a hidden database for observation, gathering information on specialists. However, "data" is like a term that includes all three and is completed as a link between the crude information and the information that can be obtained.

The data includes important components. This is the meaning for the knower, sent through a message recorded on a spatially fleeting medium: a seal, an electronic signal, a sound wave, etc.

The data must be:

a) Clear: make it clear without obscuring reality with extras;

b) Exact: and never use terms like "about.J; "quite a lot";

c) Rapid: select a programmed location to influence this choice. 'Ihe data may be clear and precise, but it will appear after the expected time, having lost its reason for being; d) Fixed: who needs it and will choose based on this data. The idea of data is also used to record data as a result of the interaction. The idea of data reduces ambiguity and can be viewed as a concrete instance of data and information. The idea of data is additionally used for items, such as information or files, which are referred to as data because they are considered "useful" as carriers of correct information or data transmission.

The data is considered a methodology in the space of assortment, differentiation of evidence, processing, association, circulation, and use in the management and utility cycle.

The growing need to look at data from a human perspective and data-driven innovation has led to the proposal of an expert area organization originally called Data Resource Management. Interpreted as data, executives have evolved into a field of concentrate previously seen as in the United States and Europe, whose hypothetical and functional entity has evolved to become a fundamental apparatus for any association that requires delivery, retrieval, collection, testing, and storage to appropriate and promotion of the use of data. Managing data through computing, organizing, and data innovation provides many possibilities, as well as what-if

and pragmatic information that enable you to organize data structures (Reuter, 2019). The data structure DS can be characterized as "a collection of interrelated parts that interact to collect, retrieve, cycle, store and disseminate data to work with the organization, control, coordination, learning and dynamics in organizations and various associations:' The most famous data structure ideas are those in which:

• Computer networks are the frameworks of the data processing parties;

• The use of computer networks by companies is, in fact, interconnected data structures;

• The development of methods for using computer networks in business includes a plan of the main parts of the data structures;

• Organizing data innovation emphasizes quality and business incentives, as well as the security of data structures in the association.

DS contains data about people, places, and those realities that help managers solve, analyze, and anticipate complex problems and solve various problems. To do this, use a template of three basic exercises:

1)information;

2) management and

3) feedback.

DS has three main capabilities to unite an organization that can transform data into information. The term executive data structure has several meanings:

• A system of people, teams, strategies, records, and exchanges that collects, approves, measures exchanges, measures, stores, retrieves, and presents information for use in organizing, planning, accounting, monitoring, and board ofdirectors for various other regulatory purposes.

• Data preparation systems to be selected by administrators;

• An organized technique to provide data from the past, present, and future, identified with internal activities and the management of external understanding. It serves to help the elements of preparation, control, and activities of the company by organizing data on the example of the appropriate time to help the leader;

• A coordinated environment between humans and machines provides data that helps the elements of activity, organization, and dynamics of an organization. An information system should provide quality information to businesses and filter them by levels of decision, or subdivide them into levels, according to the hierarchical functional levels that will use them and levels of decision that should receive the information with a summary for strategic decisions. The data structure should provide quality data to organizations and guide them to the levels of choice, or divide it into levels according to the levels of progressive practice that will use it and the levels of choice that should receive data with a summary of the options vital.

The data structure is a vital part of a partnership and is the result of three parts: Innovation, partnership, and people, where:

• Administrations: The institution is an organized and multi-level structure. Each institution has a different culture or key assumptions, qualities, and methods. Partnerships must lay the foundations to meet internal and external challenges;

• Individuals: People use data from PC-dependentframes in their work. They are necessary to enter information into the structure so that the computer can understand them.

• Innovation: innovation is how information is prepared and coordinated for people to use. PCs have supplanted innovation in manual control and can execute millions or even countless addresses per second. The data structure has the provisions ofthe information systems. In the basic information security model, there were five asset keys: people, teams, programming, information, and organizations.

• Human resources: all data frameworks need people who are end customers and specialists in information security.

• Hardware resources: all relevant gadgets used in data preparation.

• Software resources: all functional manual diagrams, called programs, that work to coordinate and control equipment, except for data preparation instruction diagrams.

• Resource data: more than a natural substance, it is an important authorized asset that must be properly monitored to help all the association's end customers.

• Resource Network: broadcast communications organizations such as the Internet, intranets, and extranets, which are vital to achieving results, "ceteris paribus': is a significant move to describe the achievements of the framework. Information, data, and facts are key components for consistency and association dynamics, but their meaning is not obvious. They structure a progressive system of differentiation of problems. What is given to one person can be data or potentially information to another. When thinking about a connection, it can be difficult to isolate obvious data, data, and information and understand their implications for your choice (Reuter, 2019).

The information can then be viewed as human-processed data. The value of the data depends on the past information about these people. Therefore, it receives information using the data directly on it. Thus, the information cannot be delivered to people, and it is firmly identified with the impression that it encodes, decodes, and distorts the data, as indicated by its attributes or according to its psychological models. The idea of information is more puzzling about data.

Knowledge is the process of understanding and masking the received data, perhaps combining it to obtain additional information. The moment he considers the relationship between the three components and creates his research, he can conclude that the information itself does not mean useful information for the dynamics, and this is only the beginning of a cycle.

The leaders' test is to transform information into data and data into information, limiting obstacles during the time dedicated to individual change. Transforming data into information and knowledge, providing information, data, and information about the consequences is not as simple interaction as it seems (Reuter, 2019).

The individual attributes that structure each person's psychological model interfere with the encoding/unravelling of these components, often causing individual distortions that can disrupt the matching process. There are contrasts between what is implicit and what it says, between what is said and what others hear, and between what they hear and what they hear, between what they understand and remember and remember, between transmissions.

People simply listen to what they need and how they need it, based on their meetings, ideal models, and previous events. There is data that people do not understand and do not see, and what data they do not see offline, data that you see but do not understand or unravel; data they see and use, data retrieval, data for calculation.

Perspective and temperament can influence the way you manage information. Educational methodologies tend to emphasize the qualities of normal, consistent, and insightful data and its manipulation to the detriment of other equally significant and insightful approaches that are identified as indirect and instinctive.

Data collection is a higher intellectual potential that takes place within a language. If you need to further explore the complexities of the environment in which they are embedded, you need to empower perception because the way of life drives a shrinking world of perception and the dream of being limited and divided and that People's data needs are constantly changing because understanding, regardless of the individual, is unexpected.

Therefore, the choice is to know that the best test is not to obtain information, data, and information but to recognize that the injury occurs in the time spent coding/unravelling and that there are ways to get rid of it.

Monitoring these and many different requests for information, data, and information barriers over time is the first step in reducing them. Encouraging solutions In a dynamic cycle, it is imperative to have information, data, and information, but these are often dispersed, separated, and deposited in the personalities of people and experience the detrimental effects of their psychological models. Around this time, the correspondence and collaboration process takes on important parts in solving some of the critical difficulties in dynamic interaction. Throughout the time spent texting, you may come to an agreement that accommodates individual strategies that vary based on persuasion rather than burden or control.

To help the nature of the authoritative choice, it is recommended to talk about the further development of the correspondence and the inclusion of people in the dynamics (Reuter, 2019).

Improving communication

Some theorists of administration, as Davenport (1998), Nonaka & Takeuchi (1997), Stewart (1998), and Sveiby (1998), suggest a new direction for communication, focused primarily on issues related to the transmission of information and organizational knowledge. The ideas of information, data, and information are strongly identified with their dynamism and are identified with the idea of correspondence.

Communication by correspondence is a group of cases in which information, data, and information are sent from the transmitter to the collector. The quality of the data is a problem of transmitting it with absolute certainty, and given the value ofthe data provided, the transfer is much more difficult. That is, it added to his understanding, considered the ramifications, even more, generating information. Consequently, the information is not said and is difficult to clarify. "Anyone who has tried to transmit information between people or meetings, you already know how difficult this task is. Communication activity occurs when people are free for themselves, trying to agree on a place that is dynamic, customizable, and belonging. To different assumptions Testing This, The view requires a few people with scientific planning, data, and interest in consensus to scoff at each of the other possible options to be an agreed-upon cumulative action scheme.

THE PERSON

1. Morals.

Morals are sure (about the qualities we should seek after), functional (because it proposes how we might assist them), and at last, supported by sanctions and institutional changes. Morality, as we imagine it, is associated with asking difficult questions about our qualities, open and public comments, and subsequent attempts to live up to them. If we find out how to live, we can say that we have decency.

This type of morality has a significant advantage in offering an answer to one of the vital questions associated with the multifaceted ways of approaching change: how to do it. Do you coordinate the different components of the change? How would you keep them in sync and avoid the changes that occur when misunderstandings occur? Morality does this because it asks the real questions.

For people, this raises the question, "How can I live my life?" Regarding institutions, he asks: "How can we lead our coexistence?" and, more generally, surprisingly, "what is the base for and what does it legitimize its reality?"

This support may not be as valuable to people in the organization, as it can add value to people who are not people in the establishment. These qualities form the basis of moral standards. They provide rules to help us change and decipher the laws that govern these funds. Morality is an essential part of this trinity Law - Moral and Institutional plans (David Wood) and combines all three into one effective technique to raise expectations and reduce impurities.

Morality does this by asking, for all equality, basic moral demands. People involved in a change of administration will generally prioritize some specific institutional or administrative change and, in addition, the implementation of the social change.

While this is an appropriate ending, a management change is certainly not an unusual set of changes to secure these closures. This should be seen as a constant course of change when we scoff at the qualities that public assistance should seek to recognize and as the best institutional method for doing so.

It reflects the idea of morality: asking ourselves difficult questions about our qualities, offering honest and public answers, and satisfying those answers. Institutions will constantly face new administrative challenges associated with changing environments or the creation of new temptations and difficulties. It should be long-lasting.

More may be needed initially to adjust to too much life change or cope with a severe pollution problem. Later, mature, you will receive new assignments from public authorities and be obliged to investigate all areas of changes presented above.

1.1. Preserving a Self-Image as an Ethical Professional

The main difference between an Ethical Person and an Unethical Person is that the former always thinks about long-term prospects and consequences for itself and its partners. If an Ethical Person builds a career, considers both employers and subordinates as partners. If it runs a business and is an employer itself, then he also has partnerships with employees.

An Ethical Leader or businessman assumes that everyone is doing one common cause and partnership; cooperation should be beneficial to both parties. An Unethical Person does not think far ahead. He keeps his focus on getting the maximum benefit right now. Where an Ethical employee will try for himself and for the whole company, an Unethical employee will look for an opportunity to do the work to a minimum, and will want to grab the benefits to the maximum. The same goes for customer relationships, whether it's your own business or work for hire.

An Ethical professional will do everything to ensure that the client is satisfied with the service and cooperation, leaves in a good mood and then recommends both the company and the specialist to everyone. And an Unethical employee will try to get rid of as soon as possible, to do everything somehow, nominally, for show, "just get it off':

Sane Ethical workers understand that buyers in stores, passengers in any type of public transport or customers in the service sector are primarily customers who give's their money for goods or services rendered and it is from this money that salaries come. Profit is formed and invoices are paid expenses.

People devoid of Ethics do not think in these categories. They are sincerely convinced that they are given too little, criminally underpaid for their "titanic" efforts, and they, poor fellows, have overworked. They can be recognized by the phrase: "As you pay me, so I work:'

Of course, there are situations when the payment in the company is really less than the average market cost of such services. Even so, Ethical and Unethical people will behave differently. An Ethical person will try to give the company more value, and then, over time, negotiate more adequate pay for this level of work. If it is not met, he will calmly leave the organization, moving to another on more favourable terms. The Unethical one will make claims, write any complaints, and throw mud at the company at all corners. Having got a new job, an Ethical person does not stop developing. He does nonstop thinking about the long-term perspective, including its own: where he will be in 5-10 years, what else he needs to learn, what knowledge, skills and abilities needs to acquire. Such an employee quite normally perceives the idea that after the end of the contract (if, for example, it was concluded for one year), will change his job for a better one. Or talk to your current employer about a pay increase without emotional manipulation and "victim position': It will give rational and easily provable arguments. For example, that during this year he acquired such and such important skills that improve the quality of its work; brought concrete measurable benefits to the company; performs now, in addition to the main ones, also a number of additional functions not specified in the contract; introduced such and such valuable suggestions, etc. Therefore, its cost for the company for this year has become objectively higher.

An Unethical Person at this time, at best, will "forge connections': look for opinion leaders and please them in every way - instead of conscientiously fulfilling his main duties. If we use the chart of psychological age sin our classification no Ethical and Unethical behaviour in business and career, we get the following picture: A psychologically adult Ethical person, whether it is a businessman or an employee of a company, considers all his actions and relationships with business partners from a long-term perspective. He is constantly growing and pumping the skills necessary to achieve even greater results.

1.2. The Ethical Behavioural Range of Values

Ethical principles are based on universal values. For example cross cultural values have shown the universality of values such as helping relatives, supporting one's group, sharing costs and benefits, respect for elders, and respect for private property. However, at any given moment in time, the basic values, depending on the context, receive a different reading and refraction in specific Ethical requirements. In this case, the context is the structure of everyday life, including the technologies that shape it. Why do we think it is important to talk about digital Ethics now?

In the end, the digital transformation processes began very recently, and many activities and territories are practically not affected by technological development. However, technologies are improving so quickly that the argument "this is not ours" is not convincing. Today there has not been any technological solution yet, tomorrow it will appear, and the day after tomorrow it will be in everyone's home or at work. The future is coming faster, and the conversation about the Ethical aspects of digitalization and the use of technology is becoming more and more relevant.

Knowledge of Ethical dilemmas arising in connection with digitalization, of the emerging rules of Ethics of digital technologies, in our opinion, is especially important for Civil servants who write laws that set mandatory rules and make other decisions that have implications for citizens and businesses. To obtain a positive effect, decision-makers must be aware of the development of technologies, understand what economic and social consequences will be caused by their application. Paying attention to the Ethical side will help to make the decision more just and thereby avoid conflicts in society between stakeholders. In addition, public administration and interaction with citizens are also being digitalized. The effectiveness of such interactions is not least dependent on whether Ethical risks have been taken into account.

The issues of Ethical application of technologies are included in the educational programs. We follow global trends; we try to look even further in order to anticipate them, in order to teach not only what is relevant now, but also what will be useful to listeners in their work in the future. We want important and useful topics, knowledge, tools to be available not only to our listeners, but also to a wide range of people. So we increase the likelihood that these questions will be asked on time, answers to them will be given promptly, consciously and after discussions, and only after that reasoned decisions will be made.

1.3. Ethical Integrative Functions

The principles of psychology are the starting points that determine the understanding of the essence and origins of the human psyche, the features of its formation, development, the mechanisms of functioning and forms of manifestations, ways of approaching its study and change. The principles accumulate in themselves the basic laws and laws operating in the field of the mental. The identification and formulation of principles is the result of long-term research by specialists. In this sense, the diversity of approaches to understanding the "psyco' is explained by the diversity of psychological schools, the originality of philosophical positions, and the bias of the research psychologist.

A great contribution to the development of the principles of psychology was made by philosophical sciences, as well as physiology, pedagogy, sociology, economics, political, science, ethics, aesthetics. All these sciences study relatively independent spheres of people's life and activities, which influence the formation and development of their psyche. It is important to understand that the laws operating in these areas have relative independence, although they experience mutual influence on the characteristics of their manifestation.

A decisive contribution to the development of the principles of psychology was made by the philosophical sciences, and above all the development of the main issue of philosophy, the general laws of dialectics, the leading categories of philosophy (quantity, quality, measure, necessity and chance, cause and effect, form and content, truth and its criteria, development, motion, interconnection, categories of matter, material and ideal), the theory of knowledge, etc. In this sense, the pluralism of approaches to understanding the variety of psychological schools is largely explained by the originality of the philosophical positions, preferences of the research psychologist. The laws operating in these areas have relative independence, although they experience mutual influence on the characteristics of their manifestation. It is important to understand this when taking into account the interaction of the laws of psychology and the social sphere of human life, the laws of their biology.

1.4. Ethical Leadership Role

The characteristics of Ethical leadership depend on the cultural context. This fact is explained by the fact that "values and norms are based on cultural characteristics and can differ significantly in different cultures: Some research has focused on identifying characteristics of Ethical leadership that are of equal importance across cultures. For example, traits such as fairness, consideration for others, and responsibility have been recognized as important in many cultures, but to varying degrees.

Since Ethical leadership is directly dependent on the cultural context and only a few studies have been conducted on the topic of Ethical leadership, and it was found out that people who work for companies in different regions define and describe Ethical leadership. To gain a deeper understanding of the issue, face-to-face meetings should be held with company employees to find out what they think about Ethical leadership in organizations. If an organization wants to develop Ethical leadership, it must purposefully seek and recruit Ethical leaders.

Research their industry reputation and ask people who know your candidate. Are candidates honest with you during interviews? Do they speak respectfully of their past employers? Meet them over lunch and study their behaviour. Ask candidates to drive you to a cafe, while assessing their willingness to accommodate and their behaviour while driving in a potentially stressful situation. You can also temporarily hire candidates for a small project; assess their communication skills and behaviour. Numerous studies conducted in various cultural contexts have shown a direct link between Ethical leadership and employee productivity improvement. Ethical leadership leads to increased productivity, employee satisfaction, loyalty to the organization, and acceptance of responsibility for completing tasks.

1.5. Embracing a Critical Morality in a Profession

A good professional must, in addition to technical and legal knowledge of the procedures that he can follow and strictly adhere to bio security concerns, dress appropriately, avoiding costumes that are incompatible with the work environment and have a polite and gentle behaviour with the client and other people who, continuously or sporadic, visit the place. When it comes to greeting and treating a client, it is imperative that zeal and respect be present in every relationship.

It is at the end of the anamnesis record that the professional has the first contact with the data information and the client's wishes. It is when, in the form of an interview, which should be done without haste, the professional collects the necessary information, which, after analyzing it, will determine the best procedure to be performed. One of the factors that most affect the extent of an adequate anamnesis is the time allotted to it. If the professional speeds up the interview, there may be corresponding deficiencies that could jeopardize the achievement of the goal. With the globalization and competitiveness of the market, and aimed at meeting the needs of customers, as well as employees, suppliers and society in general. The search for professionals who are Ethical has increased. It is clear that the practice of activity is aimed, in addition to recognition, at profit.

However, this must be achieved through fair competition, and not through the use of tricks that would tarnish the image and competence of colleagues in the profession. When it comes to the necessity and the right of a citizen to intimacy, professional secrecy becomes stricter, becomes understood as confidentiality, turning into a right-duty, that is, the right of a party generates the debt of the other. Thus, being the confidentiality of the client's rights, a specific obligation is formed for the professional.

For the treatment to be effective and the best goal is achieved, the professional needs of the client to give him certain information. This information should not remain in the public domain, as "any and all general information should be respected and used solely for the purposes for which it was disclosed': Confidentiality is due to everyone who, due to their professional activities, has access to the personal data ofthe client. The duty to keep secrets is not only Ethical, but also legal. The main purpose ofa Code of Ethics is synthesized by four elements: competence, secrecy, honesty and objectivity:

- Competence relates to the level of technical and professional training and compliance with legal norms and regulations, as well as the ability to prepare clear and complete reports;
- Confidentiality shows the degree of disclaimer that the professional has with the information entrusted to him by clients.;
- Honesty demonstrates the behaviour of professionals in the person of their class, clients and competitors, and can be dismembered in factors ranging from their social behaviour to their individual views;
- Objectivity indicates the degree of clarity that professionals have in dealing with clients and communicating information, as well as the disclosure of relevant data that can influence their decision-making.

While some elements of professional Ethics are applicable to any profession because they are universal, such as honesty, competence and responsibility, each profession should have its own Code of Ethics, considering the rights, duties, activities, duties, prohibitions and obstacles, taking into account their area of expertise, because in addition to improving the profession, it supports the client in possible doubts.

2. Shareholder Ethical Values

The Corporate Culture is able to perceive and assimilate the general structure of the organizations internal values, including Ethical Values, which are an important part of the policy and Corporate Culture of the organization and are necessary for the success of the business.

Management Ethics is a system of standards, Moral principles and values of influence on the behaviour of a person or a group of people that are guided by managers when choosing a decision, determining, from a moral point of view, what is right and what is not, what is good and what is bad. Ironically, Unethical behaviour is not uncommon in organizations. In practice, there are cases when employees lied to their superiors or colleagues, falsified report data and other documents, used drugs or alcohol in the workplace.

Social responsibility refers to the responsibility of leaders to make decisions and act in such a way that their organization contributes to the well-being of the whole society and serves its interests as well as its own. Standards for socially responsible behaviour are shaped by the values and beliefs of many external stakeholders. When making decisions, employees of the organization should be aware that their organization is part of a larger community, and take into account how its decisions and actions will look from the point of view of the global market, Government, assessed by buyers, shareholders, other interest groups and society as a whole.

When making decisions, it is necessary to predict how each of the company's alternative behaviours may affect the external environment or individual interest group. Since business practice reflects the values, attitudes and behaviours inherent in the culture of the organization, its Ethics more characterizes the organization as whole, rather than its members.

For Ethical behaviour in the workplace to become the norm for employees, an organization must make Ethics an integral part of its culture. To strengthen Ethical Values, Ethical standards must be included in the basic principles of building an organization, in the Code of Ethics and brought to the attention of members of the organization, and compliance must be linked to remuneration of employees, approval of their behaviour, attention, promotion. Environmental issues are now included as an integral part of all plans and decisions of leading companies.

The idea of Sustainable Development, when the same attention is paid to both economic growth and Environmental Protection, is gradually gaining positions in the minds of the leaders of the business world. Society no longer wants to look favourably on organizations that are focused only on making a profit and achieve this at the expense of the surrounding nature.

3. Ethical Behavioural Range of Values

Interest in wrongdoing, for instance, can be seen as the most noticeably awful disappointment of the expert as far as conduct contradictory to the common upsides of their calling. In any case, wrongdoing addresses just a glimpse of something larger of exercises that neglect to additional the common qualities that legitimize a specific calling.

Proficient wrongdoing can be viewed as the tip of an ice shelf of doubtful, exploitative, problematic, and hostile to social conduct. Regard for proficient bad conduct isn't basically about pursuing down lawbreakers. It is tied in with endeavouring to guarantee that experts satisfy the exclusive requirements that legitimize the calling's presence (Enwereuzor,2020).

The point ought not to be to focus on the most exceedingly awful types of expert conduct. Proficient conduct isn't sufficiently terrible to legitimize indictment scarcely compares to satisfying the ideal of experts maintaining the social great. Barriers might be important, even crucial; however they are not the principle game for fostering the relationship.

To put it plainly, criminal conduct will be simpler to recognize for two reasons.

- First, people taking part in such conduct will be all the more effectively apparent and all the more promptly likely to peer judgment since they will be out of the standard.
- Secondly, the more predetermined number of breaks implies that the assets of administrative and disciplinary organizations can be focused on few more segregated reprobates. With most experts falling great over the line of expected offense, the calling can join the local area and outside controllers in what will be the 'cruel quest for the couple of wrongdoers: as far as our relationship, the ice sheet will be more modest, and its tip will be minute and simpler to get at.

A basic piece of adequacy is welcoming the qualities at various focuses on the continuum into a state of harmony so the standards for each sort of conduct (the most noteworthy expert guidelines, great work, inferior work, offense, and culpability) are commonly steady comprehensively reliable. It isn't quite as straightforward as it sounds in light of the fact that various gatherings set the standards at various levels for covering however not totally steady reasons.

To have the standards at each level set by a similar body would change the nature and subvert the viability of standards at various levels. For instance, if the standards of good practice inside an institution were set by resolution, they would stop to be the standards of the institution and may be barely interpreted (Enwereuzor, 2020).

Every calling needs to have a clear enthusiasm for the distinctive standardizing frameworks included, the manner in which they cooperate, and how Moral Risk Mitigation The individuals who have worked generally perplexing and generally extended in danger moderation say that they experience this work as logically and mentally requesting, in manners they couldn't have anticipated going in.

In the mean time, others see no requirement for anything new, guaranteeing that hazard control work, where it is vital, ought to be appointed through existing line-the executives structures, with each utilitarian administrator or interaction proprietor being needed to distinguish and deal with the dangers inside their spaces.

This methodology separates at the most punctual conceivable stage-when chiefs request dangers or pain points to be named for consideration. At the point when the danger control work is appointed down the line, supervisors will by and large recognize just those dangers they know, which adjust perfectly with their practical or program regions. They are glad to uncover (Ristovski, 2017).

By embracing more conventional danger the board structures, offices are better ready to manage the dangers that are undetectable or dubious, unrepresented or under-addressed in their typical cycle stream, abnormal fit and size(along these lines not falling unmistakably inside the obligation of anybody official or office), or shared (where participation with different offices is a pre-imperative for viable mediation). Worldwide dangers are bigger scope or more elevated level dangers than the accessible control systems.

Successful activity is restricted by the shortfall of any focal control component or any lawful command or power to follow up on an adequately wide front. Unavoidably, rivals are involved; the "control" business transforms into a consistent, unique game, played against the rival's resolved to outmanoeuvre the control activity. Instances of such adversaries incorporate psychological militants, drug dealers, extortion craftsmen, programmers, and cheats.

Their size is normally questionable, bringing about genuine under-interest in charge (Enwereuzor, 2020). Instances of damages that frequently go unreported or under-detailed incorporate debasement, blackmail, drug managing; date assault; misrepresentation; betting; prostitution, many types of middle class wrongdoing, and violations inside the family dependence on worldwide settlements and intentional collaboration between offices, associations, and countries. It is not difficult to partition the work, the expenses, and the credit between the contributing gatherings.

Control tasks exist in a climate of various and contending viewpoints on the issue, frequently with next to no compelling political cycle to determine them (Enwereuzor, 2020).

Control procedures should consistently consider the adversary variations. Dominating the control match requires close checking and concentrating on the adversaries' moves and understanding and subverting their systems. To handle such dangers, an office should initially uncover them.

Methodical estimation is a basic initial phase in fostering a successful control activity. Proactive and insight work are essential for checking and discovery - for assisting with uncovering the real essence and degree of the danger and guarantee that mediations are planned around the entire of the danger as opposed to a glimpse of something larger.

4. Ethical Codes of Conduct

All companies have a fundamental obligation to adapt to the basic conditions of both the state and the social environment in which and for which they operate. In a rapidly changing world and constantly growing competitive pressures, it becomes more difficult to find clear guidelines for yourself and for the employees for whom the company is responsible. For this reason, and through Code of Conduct, we would like to establish and apply binding general guidelines of conduct (Code of Conduct) based on Laws and standards for both managers and employees.

The main goal of a Code of Conduct should be to create reliable high-level jobs with sufficient wages for as many people as possible. For this reason, ensuring and developing business, in a healthy atmosphere and the success of the company should be the main goal Wanting to fulfil socio-political obligations to the people who live and work in the area of the economy, in the communities and countries accepted business practices and comply with the rules of fair competition.

Rejecting corruption and bribery as outlined in the relevant UN Convention and the acceptance of unfair advantages through the use of the managing position in the company. In addition to meeting legal requirements and standards, the expectations and interests of clients should be the priority and guiding principle. With regard to the practical implementation of the BENNING corporate philosophy, safety at work and health, environmental protection, as well as the quality of the products and services provided must take absolute priority.

Generally, an Ethical Code of officials and employees of companies with State participation may appear, regulating their behaviour and statements in the blogosphere. As practice shows, corporate standards, let's call them so, a certain code of honour and Ethics, is an effective management tool. It is not for nothing that such codes have become widespread world practice. The perception of top officials, governors and top managers of State-owned companies is an investment, and even to some extent a matter of National Security.

Given the relevance that Social and Environmental Impacts are acquiring in recent years in the strategic direction of organizations, there is a tendency to develop business codes of conduct of different origins. In this sense, several types can be distinguished:

• Developed by individual organizations independently;

• Promoted by international intergovernmental organizations (eg DECD guidelines);

• Negotiated and approved by different social partners such as companies, NGOs, unions, etc. (eg Ethical Trading Initiative, UN Global Compact). The adoption of Codes of Ethics or Conduct can serve various purposes, such as:

• Internal management tool to declare the Values and Ethical standards of the organization;

• Way to influence the practices of its partners or global businesses;

• Means of informing customers and suppliers of the principles followed in the development and manufacture of their products.

These Codes of Ethics or conduct are very important since once signed they become a legal agreement between the employee and the employer. These codes do not constitute a certification system since they do not follow certain standards (ISO, EMAS standards) but are limited to collecting in an internal document a series of values for information purposes both for employees and for customers or suppliers.

Thus, it does not include an evaluation system, process development, implementation or other procedures that allow verifying its execution and results in the internal structure of the organization. The content of these codes refers to the protection of fundamental, labour and Environmental rights and practices against corruption and bribery.

Likewise, they may contain specific guidelines in the relations between the employee and the organization, establishing sanctions in the event of the performance of certain behaviours that go against the values and principles stipulated by the company. However, although a company can establish Codes of Conduct unilaterally, they cannot go against the law, social dialogue or collective bargaining. Limits to the content of these codes, considering that it exceeds the power of direction and supervision of the company and violates the rights to privacy and dignity of the worker, his freedom of expression and information are:

a) The duty of prior communication to HR of the participation as speakers in external courses or seminars;

b) The obligation to obtain prior authorization from the company for any dialogue or contact with journalists and the media of any kind and for all disclosure and information about the entity in any type of media or social network, including news, reports, economic and / or financial data, accounting data, business objectives, logos, photocopies, etc.;

c) The obligation to obtain the prior authorization of the HR management and the person in charge to intervene in conferences, congresses, conferences, meetings, seminars, courses and other similar events, as well as classes in universities or educational institutions, both those of punctual character such as those that are taught permanently, both public and private, either onerous or free.

Therefore, these stipulations would exceed what is legally allowed and, consequently, will be declared void. Codes of conduct can be a good starting point in the strategic management process of organizations, especially in terms of corporate values and mission, since they must be the consensual basis on which the social responsibility of organizations is sustained.

However, they are only binding if they fit in with and do not contradict the rules governing labour relations.

5. Inspirational Ethics Code

The activity of any company, like a fabric made of threads, consists of economic relations between different groups of people. These are customers and management, employees and suppliers, shareholders and competitors. In order for the result of their contacts to be "smooth': without knots and holes, everything should be foreseen and the rules of the game should be stipulated for your team. It is extremely important to have a clearly defined philosophy of interaction between all business entities. Moreover, the larger the organization, the more obvious the need for a Corporate Code becomes. If in micro-companies everything is decided at the level of personal communications, then it is not so easy to quickly, competently and easily introduce a new employee of a large enterprise.

Moreover, a well-established, published version of the company's Professional Code of Ethics will nullify the distortion of these standards. And in the case of oral transmission from one employee to another, such a risk still exists.

The first thing for which a document should be created is the function of design and transfer of Corporate Culture.

With the help of the Corporate Code, the new employee is socialized in the team. If for some reason the employee does not share the philosophy of the company, it becomes possible to identify such a fact and filter it out at the stage of the applicant.

The second, most pragmatic of all, the task of the professional "Moral Code" is to improve the management processes in the company. Typically, the document declares the principles governing the behaviour of personnel, relationships with customers and management, the employee's responsibility to the company and vice versa.

All this helps to minimize service conflicts, remove corruption in the team, and rationally use the company's resources. Thus, the

Corporate Code helps to achieve greater efficiency in production and management. The image bonuses of the document are no less significant.

Service Code of Ethics has become an indispensable standard for doing business around the world for decades. This is an indicator of the openness and integrity of the company. Trust is the key to success. The most frequently used principle of constructing a document is where declarative ideas and practical content are distinguished. The first, ideological, part includes the mission, the fundamental values and goals of the company, as well as the requirements of the leadership.

The goal is the organizations aspirations from the point of view of its own development, a kind of "horizons of success": In contrast, a mission statement is a description of what social contribution the company makes in achieving its goals.

The mission can be framed verbatim or vice versa - presented in the form of a short slogan. In the first part of the document, it is permissible to present a message from the organization's management, to disclose the history of the company in a thesis, to present corporate heroes (there are outstanding personalities in any team, and their atypical, but significant actions will come in handy here).

The Code of Conduct of Procter & Gamble (P&G) is almost a benchmark. Here are some ofthe values described in it:

- A team of the world's best specialists;
- The owner's attitude to the property of the company (as to his own); striving to ensure the long-term successful activities of the company, to fulfil the assigned tasks, to increase labour efficiency;
- Honesty and openness in relations between employees; compliance with the letter of the law; decision-making based on complete information and its reasonable assessment, taking into account possible risks;
- Striving to be the best in performing assigned tasks, improving the quality of work; exercising leadership in their field;

• The mutual trust in relationships between colleagues, customers and users. The second part of the Corporate Code contains information that is more applicable in practice. It will be useful here to list and disclose the fundamentals of personnel policy and the principles of payroll. A great incentive to be a part of the company will be the description of the social package for its employees.

Do not forget to place a scheme for resolving work conflicts between different participants in the production process. State the requirements for the style of relationships between employees of the company. Mention staff social responsibility, house rules and workplace safety.

5.1. General Guidelines of Inspirational Ethical Codes

It seems that it is only in our time that special attention has been paid to Corporate Culture. But this is not the case. Even in the Middle Ages, people united along professional lines and followed corporate rules. The development of Corporate Culture has always had the main task - to unite the team to effectively achieve the required results. It is found out what is the main difference between the Corporate Code and corporate ethics, what corporate ethics is, and what is its main advantage for business in 2022.

The Corporate Code of a company is called a complete list of corporate rules, common goals and values. Most often, this is a large document in which all the bylaws ofthe company are spelled out to the smallest detail. It can include: • The history and mission of the company;

• The structure by department;

• The procedures in the company (hiring, adaptation, employee assessment, training, dismissal rates);

• The internal regulations (working hours, sick leave, vacation, holidays, workplace);

• The company policy (data confidentiality, security rules). Corporate Ethics is one of the important sections of the Corporate Code.

Fundamentals of corporate Ethics

The corporate Ethics of the company is based on common values, traditions and norms of behaviour of employees. Its base is made up of:

1) The values of the company, which are shared by every employee.

2) Following the general mission of the company.

3) Belief in the success of the company.

4) Productive collaboration between employees, allowing to achieve common goals.

5) Career development: trainings, courses, professional development.

6) Motivation, performance evaluation, reward.

7) Code of business conduct, clothing style.

The combination of these characteristics constitutes the Ethical basis. Each employee, entering the company, follows these rules and thereby forms the Corporate Ethics of the company.

Back in 2000, the French company l`Oreal issued its own Corporate Code of Ethics. 14 years later, the company issued the third edition of the code, available in 45 languages. Already in 2019, the company was named one of the world's most ethical companies for the tenth time. L`Oreal's Code of Ethics covers quality standards in product development, research, marketing, logistics and working conditions. The annual celebration of the Ethics Day has already become a tradition for the company. During the day, each employee can ask questions to the management and get answers to them. On Ethics Day, it is customary to remind employees of the main ethical principles of the company: honesty, respect, courage and transparency. The example of L`Oreal proves that corporate ethics works to develop a company's brand.

In 2020, when an employee chooses a company, and not vice versa, a Code of Ethics may be the factor that will tip the scales in your favour. It happens that the work of your company outwardly looks flawless, like the smooth running of an expensive watch mechanism. Each department solves its part of the work, the management and middle managers are involved in strategic planning and decision-making, and the ordinary staffs diligently performs the tasks assigned to it. But at the slightest hint of a crisis, such a business risks falling apart like a house of cards. In modern realities, the absence of a set of beliefs and rules in a company that regulates production culture and ethics becomes dangerous. It usually takes the form of a Corporate Code.

ENVIRONMENT

1. The Problem

1.1. Facing a crisis is widespread civilization

Fighting for a different worldview of coincidence of relations with the Earth as the consent of a society to respect and protect everything that exists has life. Again, we must wait for a response, and it is this change promises a good start for considering options. As a typical perspective seemed, the standard of self-development is evolving. It will generally rule the human brain, apt to undermine the balance of physical-synthetic and Ecological shredding in the planet's biosphere, taking risks with many living things.

Life dates precisely from millions or billions of long periods of transformative events, undermined by a more modern and extreme creation. This absence, whose sources it does not distinguish, or in addition, is perceived with the help of its constituent components.

Sachs (1993), the population as a whole was expected to double in size until the end of the 20th century, so this is a fundamental and impartial advance of human culture to reduce social contrasts. People who benefit from inconsistent asset allocation globally must give up some green space.

They attract the people who need them. Through long periods of destruction, natural depreciation, and the extraction of limited assets in the financial and formative development in the gathering of abundance and unstable speed, causing changes in the Environment, are compromising the stability of the planet and the resistance of the species, for example, with organizations operating at twice the speed. Unilateral, transforming politically sanctioned into real organizations (Ehrlich, 2013).

This vision:

a) Progress towards a socially just turn of events and respect for nature is based on adequate responses to the emergency by organizations that, to varying degrees, affect the three groups of nations: East, South, and North, as well as the global framework.;

b) The future of developing countries depends on their ability to discover successful scenarios in public and private spheres to establish relationships between the social the financial and the economy.

c) The Prosperous North manifests itself as a model, but not practical for the expansion of the entire planet, the number of assets that society requires to use and the amount of waste that it produces and throws into nature. Research is an absolutely necessary method to advance towards a more intelligent sustainability in the planetary scale;

d) Economic development is fundamental but inadequate to ensure a turn of events; development can support a turn of events on a genuine problem. A broad development method for concentrated development; Humankind have to go against the possibility of extinguish the civilization devastating the planet and Biosphere of life.

e) The claims about purchasing power, devastating arable land, forests and living species or a social appropriation program;

f) Modern development in the North and its counterparts in the South are described by a gigantic misuse of the Earth's assets, which implies the destruction of the metropolitan nature. This waste is a kind of deterrent to advancement. These assets, kept through a organizations could finance social spending or speculation while having inexhaustible assets.

The need is to combine science and methods for the needs of development, within the framework of the principles of intelligence, natural and continuous biotechnological progress, to facilitate advanced modern civilization in the creation of an undeniably wide range of modern elements associated with the many weather disasters.;

Based on effective environmental improvement examples, we summarize this approach. Create for a broader range, a design framework planned according to conventional biological systems meeting three essential standards:

- Social value;
- Natural intelligence;
- Financial education. In addition, for Sachs (1993), a significant commitment is to characterize the global responsibility of the various groups of nations to establish and manage procedures to advance towards environmental protection.

2. Deep Ecology

Deep ecology, proposed by Norwegian thinker Arne Ness in 1973, reacts to the prevailing view of the use of conventional assets. Arne Ness follows the tradition of environmental philosophy as seen by Henry Thoreau in Walden and Aldo Leopold in his Earth Ethics. Arne Ness falls into environmental philosophy, considered by Henry Thoreau, proposed by Walden and Aldo Leopold in his work Ethics of the Earth.

It is called deep ecology because it demonstrates a reasonable qualification against the prevailing world view. All the problems that arise from destruction are directly identified with the human turn of events.

Hiding behind his achievements (BOFF, 2004, p. 22). Paraphrasing Boff (2004), we can say that creating the fastest processor at any time or creating a machine that replaces the gardening work of 1000 people. The people's greed for it is not satisfied with living with it. It offers enough to believe that it is an option to do so, removing the causes of progress and advancement. He has more than meets his property status material products in exchange for destroying the normal, which is delicious, essential, yet different.

Therefore, is it an exception to regular organic control that the individual avoids the principles of nature to regulate the number of living people? For Boff (2004), this is known as his collaboration in the trap of life since you wonder how free the mystery of life on Earth is.

Life on Earth can exist without people, but people cannot live without other lives to care for and trade in matter and energy. The connection between people and other living creatures of the Earth, who do not like their extraordinary lack of modesty to satisfy their outdated nature, will eventually destroy various living groups of animals or indirectly affect achieving your goals unnecessarily.

Reasons for progress and improvement are hidden from the public and the conditions for the domain of the raw natural material for transformation in exchange for the destruction of nature.

A rapidly growing population forms this structure of tight-fisted people that does not influence their expansion in the planet's space. For example, a person dominates its live. Over time, though many others can steer clear of most fatal variables before facing catastrophic circumstances. Consequently, this is a particular case of standard organic control, when a person deviates from the norms of nature to adjust the number of residents (Ehrlich, 2013).

Life on Earth can exist without people, but a person cannot live without other living things, which must be cared for and treated with care and energy. The connection between people and other living beings, has led to the destruction of various animals, alive or indirectly destroying their habitat, what necessarily affect their existence and reproduction.

The types of life in the world demonstrate a lack of understanding of the fragile line that follows the average balance, which also recommends the demand to maintain this balance to spread the everyday Environment on Earth (Ehrlich, 2013).

3. Environment and Human Behaviour

The current world viewed on environmental problems gives a more visible degree and understanding of what is happening to the climate where living matter is found and affected.

The misfortune, the devastation, and the two-handed use of conventional resources are increasingly manifested against human culture, causing one-sided ecological characteristics, causing depletion and nature.

The reason for maintainability is that people are seen as a feature of nature that can carry out their activities protecting the climate in which they live. In the history of the development, it can be noted that the person under consideration becomes, from the beginning, where the conflict of the old Cartesian worldview and the new worldview - sustainability is involved.

Considering the limits that affect the research and its implications, it remains within its purpose. Still, it offers new thinking to influence the fight against the preparation of natural mindfulness in dynamic development (Ehrlich, 2013).

The actions existing today by the climate are not consistent with those of conscious people. We have to be focused on meaningful activities to limit the implications for this reason. Finding the reasons that make the conscious activity of the generator of perspectives and cycles to mitigate environmental problems is fundamental, given the irregularity of people aware of the presence of natural activity. It is not enough to cure the disease. It must be prevented. This is important to investigate what has been lost and restore the tendency to regain balance to keep up with it and obtain an average balance of biological systems.

Looking at the similar limits of the search for harmony, we can refer to different examples of confusion. Shared vision and submission to the real world, but something is wrong. It is necessary to supplant the Cartesian-Newtonian worldview, united by a positivist convention, which governs our lives (Ehrlich, 2013).

For this world, changes must taken considering that the emergency that affects humanity. Teaching plays a vital role dedicated to environmental management. Training young people and adolescents, integrating Ecological and Human qualities, emphasizing the feeling of daily rehearsals with the hypothesis raised in the classroom, fostering a culture of support, a culture of harmonious connection between people and between them and nature.

Pursuing practical advancement seems idealistic, but idealistic thoughts are to make what you dream, and the dream is to build trust. It is necessary to extract reality, stop chattering on solid ground, and take a step (Ehrlich, 2013).

The Environment and development must cease to be apart to become a partnership relationship. The central theme of this problem becomes the demand for a silent connection between the nature of the climate and financial development. It is expected that what activities are equipped to protect the Environment. Discovering the secret of cognition and its ability to carry out informed and presented actions responsible for the propagation of problems and significant environmental improvements. We must develop a conscious mentality in people; natural care is not an activity to mitigate the Environmental effects (Ehrlich, 2013).

Understanding the premise of creating activities is vital to contact attentive people to have a reliable point of view from their vision. Finding a factor for action was a trick much more than just conscience. If mindfulness were great enough, concern for the environmental issue, as is clear would be in different parts of the natural mindfulness multiplier.

Perhaps most people did not see the seriousness of the problem or don't want to see the truth that it honestly touches and ends with nature. A person with an environmental conscience does not motivate to monitor a natural problem, it should be encouraged to foster the development of the prospects that an equivalent can cure or prevent biological damage. Finding a direction requires an investigation that focuses on a separate heading of subtleties that may be associated with its true goal.

It is essential to ask a troubling question: why are there many people, despite being naturally attentive, but without common sense, have perspectives that make the steps environmentally sustainable? Reflecting on the transformative history of the human idea, one may notice that the contemplator becomes forever, where he balances the conflict of the old Cartesian worldview and the new worldview of resilience. For the problem being analyzed, natural issues do not bother enough people, so they act; there is no inspiration or individual desire to induce environmental activism.

Mindfulness does not change people's views on environmental issues. Environmental discernment and awareness actions can emphasize feelings in humans that have been honed to elevate progressions important to achieve maintainability. Given the boundaries that affect research and the implications of this work, she remains within her intended purpose. Still, she does not offer new thoughts to influence how to transcend the training of natural mindfulness in dynamic development (Likhotal, 2014).

4. Environment Behavioural Paradigms

The moment a person awakens to a new worldview, it is Newton and Descartes' "thoughtless origin for an all-encompassing and biological view;' in the pursuit of a vision of relationships and does it is vital for everyday existence: fundamental changes in our thinking, discernment, and qualities. Research explains what a worldview is. In its work "The structure of scientific revolutions; "

Thomas Kuhn gives two meanings of the word "worldview":

The first has to do with sentimentality, qualities, and techniques used by citizens;' which established the discipline by which an organization coordinates with itself and maintains the location of your connections.

The second is derived from the primary method for reference models, the arrangement of questions taken and held as duplicates and replacing certain principles when dealing with various questions from moral science. By analyzing the ideas, one can pick up a fundamental belief that is broadly similar to the research here discussed

The refusal to: "degrade the Earth to a progression of ordinary assets or a deposit of unrefined physical and complex components," as Boff said. The rationale: in the search for a new worldview, the desire to use new science and innovation in nature, defending the solution of the idea of worldview proposed by Kun.

Created by the disrespectful view of the logical rebellion that Copernicus, Descartes, Bacon, Newton spoke of, Galileo portrays the world as a machine governed by numerical laws. The development of the human idea, the exposure of complex cycles that reveal the work of living organic beings, did not have the opportunity to subvert the Cartesian worldview. Lavoisier, William Blake, Goethe, Kant, and Khatlon separated living organic entities as self-propagation and self-association saw the coordination between their meetings and the planet (Arora, 2018).

Boff describes: "Everything was full of reverence and love because they considered that things were simply idle creatures, however significant and brilliant they were. In various articulations of the Great Mother, the land was the developed land, and the home was regarded as a living organic being. It cannot be abused or persecuted.

In any case, in revenge for storms, lightning, droughts, flames, tremors, and volcanic eruptions, a person felt respect and admiration even with Mother Earth. As the creator points out, this inclination has never been wholly lost in humanity. Today, this trend dates back to the supposed exploration of Earth.

Regard Earth as "Gaia;' a living, in the way that is coordinated and discretely adapted, invariably delicately and consistently paraphrased, as hypothesized by NASA researcher Lovelock (1991). Fundamentally speaking, the properties of a life form or living frame are properties of the whole that neither side has. If parsed into separate components, these properties are destroyed.

The shift from robotic thinking to fundamental thinking prompts us to reflect on the practical reasoning that has led people to accept this question as a single reliable reality; all miracles are optional inductions. For fundamental reasons, matter can be found in another structure; like energy, the issue is not just material but settled energy, full of complex connections.

It even expresses that matter, as the philology of word suggests, is a mother with all equals, including existence, which is the self-association of the value of the advanced period and improvement of science. They created development models incompatible with the natural balance that existed during Western civilization, which finally broke this Ecological catastrophe (Arora, 2018).

The Cartesian worldview - "rationalism;' "sanity;' or "Cartesian logic" - is a way of thinking that has emerged in the current century XVII was described in detail by the French logician Descartes (1596-1650). For Descartes, science is deductive and specific information is intelligent like arithmetic. Inference, or reasoned statement, refers to the exposure that moves from the general to the particular and allows you to arrive at a specific solution from a combined group of recommendations, like a request. Descartes's strategy is to divide questions and reflections into parts, which are coordinated causal relationships. Thus, everything is perceived from the interruption and consideration of individual proposals. Descartes demonstrates the reality of the above by showing the causal relationships that govern the research subject. So, for Descartes, the equilibrium appears immediately, like the circumstances and the logical results.

The Cartesian way of thinking was the focus of mediation in nature, which is now seen as "knowing it for its use, control, and management," based on human power over nature. It emphasizes that understanding standards-based things is a necessary resource for managing them. Descartes said that science must become aware of human instinct and the world (Likhotal, 2014).

Nature is seen as a cruel world, devoid of all dynamism, innovation in general, all the capacity of any soul, all compassion or disgust, all heat or freshness, all tone, taste, and smell, so that the world is entirely mechanical, without a secret, without life, and without maturity.

Cartesian logic influenced the reasoning because the climate was simply a thoughtless origin of nature. It is meaningless and completely defenceless against human abuse. In refinement, accurate information and any miracle can be obtained simply through perception and experimentation. Unlike pragmatists, they argue that explanation, reality, and rational thought are acquired through experience. In this methodology, a logical hypothesis is a consequence of experimentation.

The purpose is that the analysis plans to test ideas, validate them, and reproduce them. Using an inductive strategy, the introduction of suspicions about the subject leads to the truth. Despite its realism, induction ensures that information begins with the experience of the faculties or vibrations that structure understanding (sight, hearing, touch, taste, smell). Belonging creates an atmosphere of paraphrased thoughts. Encounters are seen by palpable intuition and the tendencies and structuring of ideas in memory in the light that it is a social opportunity to form thoughts.

The Englishman Francis Bacon (1561-1626) was an exemplar empiricist, the first to support the inductive technique for analytical research, obtaining information from people to reach common knowledge with profound energy for logical experiments, defending the value of research tests. His maxim was to be capable, in his opinion, that analytical information is a viable tool to manipulate reality. Empirical regulation focused on functional science, dependent on experimental inductive techniques, generalized laws based on the perception of repetition of events with stable qualities (Likhotal, 2014).

This is the assumption that the logical information used to control the reality prepared for this science can also be used to dominate and control nature. In contrast, the information offered as the subject of individual encounters, perceived exclusively by each person, encourages people to foster individuality. In this sense, personality was more of a priority than culture.

Meetings with a clear interest and financial abuse causing a clear adverse effect of human activities in nature were seen only as a good side. They would cause a more notable increase in funding for these particular meetings.

Isaac Newton (1642-1727) used a technique that combined common sense, induction, determinism, and system to contribute to his ideas. In the early last century 20th century, when it fell into decline, the constraints of the Newtonian model were produced simply by using the hypothesis of relativity and the quantum hypothesis, which have improved our way of thinking. Kantian's perspective is "basic:' With the current upheavals of the 17th and 18thcenturies, the advent of the steam engine has created an association between science and innovation, causing significant climate change.

Positive thinking is the power of motivation to change the world. Enlightenment was the major crisis proposed by Immanuel Kant (1724-1804) in his Assessment of Pure Reason. The analysis refers to the Kantians. Analysis, mindset wins at this point. The individual who occupies basic and autonomous characteristic positions has an independent point of view and simply recognizes what is believed to be evident after thinking about reality (Likhotal, 2014).

It is believed that since the Enlightenment, people began to have an independent mind, not allowing it to be controlled and manipulated. The analysis influenced the consideration by presenting a natural primary position, separating it from the willing acceptance of realities.

What propelled researchers and inspirers, especially to the 20th century, opened the possibility of scrutinizing the prevailing speculations and logical patterns, creating associations between them and the moment of a natural emergency. This mindset made it possible to develop new ideal models for solving the problem of one natural disaster that happened and preventing others.

Comte (1798-1857)was its leading representative of positivism, which emerged as a post-Kantian way of thinking in the 19th century, during the transition to the modern insurgency. This commandment turned the "legend of scientism" into a "legend of scientism," extolling science and logical technique for which all information is conceivable and perfect. He is confident in the benefits that science and innovation will adapt to the current turmoil of business progress.

Positivism denied the heartbreaking social consequences of industrialization, guaranteed the authenticity of business, and explicitly accepted the presence of industrial visionaries and managers. The reasonable, logical investigation and the human soul must realize the inconceivability of receiving direct terms about its starting point, the universe's fate, and unravel the problem (Likhotal, 2014).

The difference lies in the knowledge of miracles through their laws, thanks to which science exists. Positivism profoundly influenced the reasoning because Ecology introduced a way of thinking about progress, perceived as a specialized logical progression and gathering of material goods, which was won over by the repairable turn of events style created by the polluted space of nature. Innovation and science were devices for the domination of nature by man, which could give an idea of ordinary phenomena. He recognized the emergence of new logical speculations, tested on analytical information rather than directly, that allow for new methodologies and new environmental methodologies.

4.1. Building new cultural, social, political, and economic values

Preliminary political events - most of them looking for votes, trying to convince people to work for nature - are a small piece of waste from the city destined for reuse. The moment the changes are past governments projects, they are ignored or rejected. Another program is launched as environmental issues quickly highlight natural matters. Finding the reasons that cause the conscious activity of the generator of mentalities and cycles that can begin to mitigate biological problems is essential, given the irregularity of people who are aware ofthe presence and absence of prolonged environmental activity.

Capturing nature is a terrible thing. Education plays a strategic role in the environmental management process, teaching children and young people the human and Ecological values, highlighting the meaning of daily practice with theory initiated in the classroom, leading to a culture of sustainability, a culture of harmony, coexistence between people and between them and nature. The search for sustainable development seems romantic.

Still, romantic ideas try to build what you dream of, creating hope. This is the desire to abstract from concrete reality, to stop wandering on dry land. Developing sustainability means focusing on something other than production. Still, it means thinking and solving minor problems to get away from the proposed natural, logical process or finding answers in nature to solve problems. We must go back to basics to rethink the human way of life.

See what was lost to accommodate the missing piece or re-participate in Earth's life cycle. Sustainable development chooses the creative initiative of people as its primary resource and material and spiritual well-being as its main objective. Communities that perform well, even in conditions of poverty, also have ingenious coping strategies (Likhotal, 2014).

What activities have been organized to ensure the climate protection? It is expected to reveal the secret of consciousness and its ability to take conscious, represented, and responsible actions to spread agreements and tremendous natural improvements? You can't just plant trees every year in seven days of weather and love the moment like it has a massive impact on people and the weather. We must develop people's mindfulness, natural attention, and proactively to mitigate the environmental effects.

Understanding what inspires a production activity is vital to reaching out to caring people so they can reconcile your point of view with your point of view. The discovery of the activity factor was a tool much more than just awareness. If mindfulness is large enough, concern for the environmental issue, as is clear from the organization, would arise in different parts of the natural mindfulness multiplier. Suppose every person with an Ecological conscience lacks the motivation to continue working on an environmental issue. In that case, they are in the right place to foster the prospects that an equivalent person can cure or prevent natural damage.

Persons are fundamental to protect and preserve the united universe of people and nature as used to be in particular (Likhotal, 2014). The struggle for a different worldview of the coincidence of relations with the Earth as the consent of society to consider and save everything that exists has life. Once again, we must wait for a response, and it is this change that augurs a good start for pondering the options. The people who benefit from the inconsistent global asset swap must give up some of the green space they own to those who need it.

During long periods of destruction, environmental degradation, and the extraction of limited assets in monetary and formative development in the accumulation of abundance and inconsistent speed, causing environmental changes, undermining the stability of the planet and the resistance of species with organizations working at double rate, for example, unilateral, becoming real organizations politically sanctioned with racial segregation. Sachs notes that the vision is:

a) Changing the socially impartial turn of events and respect for nature depends on adequate responses to an emergency by the institutions, which affect in varying degrees the three assemblies of nations: East, South, and North, as well as to the global framework.

b) The final destiny of developing countries depends on their ability to open the powerful scenarios of the public and private spheres to manage the relationship between the social and money, from one point of view and another, between the financial subject and nature

c) The Prosperous North is manifested as a model, but not achievable for the expansion of the entire planet, the number of goods that society requires to use, and the amount of waste that it produces and removes in nature, so the request is systems need to move towards a more real development on a planetary scale;

d) Economic development is essential, but not in the most minor adequate to ensure a turn of events. Development can support a turn of events or a genuine question of a helpless turn that invokes subjective rules.

e) The needs are unmistakable and theoretical, moral, political, social, social, and financial, access to a package of arable land or a program of social circulation;

f) Modern Human progress in the North and its imitation in the South is described by a gigantic misuse of the Earth's goods, which implies the destruction of metropolitan nature. These waste drive cutting-edge modern developments in creating an inexorably wide range of modern elements related to multiple climate disasters.;

g) Based on examples of effective environmental improvement, we summarize this approach and establish, through testing on a larger scale, a creation framework that is planned according to the everyday Environment and meets three core standards:

1) Social value;

2) Bio-monetary viability, and

3) efficiency.

Likewise, for Sachs (1993), the essential obligation is to characterize the global commitment of the various assemblies of Nations to create and implement progress in environmental improvement. The North must make a more visible effort, committing to fight for economic improvement on a global scale, measured in three dimensions: • Reducing the use of non-renewable energy sources;

• Avoiding lifestyle changes:

• The desire to create a component that guarantees a positive net promotion of monetary and specialized assets, from North to South, rather than the commercial viability of access to science and innovation in developing countries (Arora, 2018).

4.2. Economic Development and Environmental Awareness

Organizations have begun collaborating to limit the adverse effects of pollution and demand environmental commitments. Global good practices and agreements have had the opportunity to prosecute violators of reasonable emission standards. Economic interests can be combined with environmental ones. Still, financial arguments govern and guide most public administrations. Everything must obey them and that nature is outside the economy.

People are essential to a business idea, so the economy should be viewed as a property of nature. Environmental problems must be considered one of the most severe challenges facing the business world in this first decade.

Organizations must advance on this central issue, act quickly and proactively, and not leave a receptive posture. In environmental awareness, it is essential to instruct and implement the idea of climate as an accomplice, not as a limitation of financial activities.

This awareness was the understanding that it is essential to make profits, but now with a vision of government assistance, without damaging the climate, instructing the buyer here and there to improve environmental conditions (Ursul, 2018). For extreme protectionists, especially in agricultural countries, the development path accelerated income growth through appropriate natural approaches. It seems that the quality search now focuses more on the organization of environmental risk, environmental quality.

Total quality is a suitable tool for the job. All activities and practices must be considered to assess a company's ability to respond to a waste problem and significantly contribute to climate and environmental performance. Accurately characterized and properly implemented to reduce and control the business climate impact. The activity must cover the Environment for the successful evacuation of the waste generated.

The quality of the Environment is a prerequisite for physical, complex, natural, social, monetary, and mechanical improvement to ensure the ecological soundness of the connections in the biological system in which exercise is necessary for the association.

The search for natural environmental productivity returns us to a state known for manageability. For the egregious protectionists, especially in agricultural countries, the path to improvement was to accelerate wage growth through conventional methodologies. It seems that the quality search now focuses more on the association between natural hazards and environmental quality.

Environmental quality is a fundamental prerequisite for physical, material, average, social, monetary, and mechanical progress to guarantee the continued safety of associations within the natural framework in which exercise is fundamental to the association. Absolute quality is the right tool to take care of Everything (Ursul, 2018).

To explore the organization's ability to respond to the problem of waste and to undertake significant commitments to environmental responsibility, any type of movement and method must be considered. They are accurately described and properly implemented to reduce and control the impact of the business environment. The action must cover the Environment for the fruitful care of the waste generated.

The nature of the climate is essential for physical, stunned, average, social, financial, and mechanical improvement to ensure the ecological sufficiency of the associations in the organic structure in which exercise is vital for belonging. The search for everyday ecological utility returns us to a state known for its sensitivity (Ursul, 2018).

Accreditation solves a natural problem, especially in those areas that are coordinated with the coordination of actions provided for in current regulations. However, for some companies, biological confirmation is a tool to advertise adapt to new circumstances and pressures from environmental activists, although this aspect of supporting various types of climate pollution remains flawless.

The democratization of social activity concerning the exhibition economy is problematic. On the one hand, the closer the dynamic circle is to the inhabitant, the more remarkable possibilities of social control; on the other hand, we are following the development of the unions and business organizations promoting the choice of the neighbourhood.

It is the mystery of the majority rule system, environmental control, biodiversity conservation, natural learning of organizations. The World Commission on Environment and Development, established in 1983, emphasizes that "potential improvement is an improvement that solves the present problems without compromising people's ability to meet their own needs in the future:' This idea of environmental corruption will be discredited when deciphered by various social actors to be seen as a port of transition for the components of the world's power throughout our average time or as a system of development and market profit.

A society that respects the Environment is one that:

a) Conserve biodiversity and the networks that support emotional life;

b) It ensures the practical use of inexhaustible assets and limits the distortion of volatile assets;

c) Strives to stay within biological support systems. In 1972, the Club of Rome, called Growth Cuts, focused on analyzing how they create and maintain their climate destruction.

Progress alone does not exist, but the general public stops at the improvement they need and need. It recommends that a possible society believe enough for them and for the beings of the biological systems in which it is found, accepting that nature can supplant it.

Gradually, the organization shows itself prepared to anticipate new inclinations and some plans.

The progress has been dramatically accelerated due to evolving eco-balance and performance considerations within cut-off points. These changes lead to the fulfilment of various limits, for example, the contrasts between fun, warmth in friendships and empathy for the follow-up in desperate or underestimated circumstances, the formation of compensatory measures, and social attention.

Ground controllability standards:

a) Build a sustainable society;

b) Respect and care for local living beings;

c) Improve the nature of human existence;

d) Support the imperative and diversity of the Earth;

e) Stay within the limitations of the ability to help planet Earth;

f) Changing individual attitudes and practices;

g) Enable networks to cope with current circumstances;

h) Create a public building for improvement and conservation;

i) Form a worldwide association. Manageability hints at the need to expand the limits of earthly assets and imagination using innovation to limit the use of petroleum products, inexhaustible and non-renewable investments, reduce waste and pollution by conserving energy, support, and strategies for advance in the use of materials from rich and defenceless nations and intensify the search for innovations for the economic and skilful use of goods to improve the metropolis, the country, and modernity, as well as to characterize cooperative principles for natural trust.

j) Advances in the network recommend several examples of social connections. Its proposal depends on the firmness, resilience of the local associations, and their strong inspiration, qualities, and habitual interests so that each local region can participate effectively in the development of its path.

k) Expect mechanical progress as a way of ensuring harmony between financial aspects within modern society, then, at this point, it tends to be seen as a vital condition for the consistency and "sustainability' of the improvement cycle.

Manageability. The space tends to reduce extreme fixation in metropolitan areas, controls the destruction of fragile biological systems, promotes horticulture and ranch maintenance using current regenerative procedures for small ranchers; explore the possibilities of decentralized industrialization alongside a new era of ecological advancements, and create a natural storage organization and biosphere to ensure biodiversity. When it comes to natural mindfulness, it will look for a practical turn of events, a dream that, for those who know it, will understand how to evolve given the climate in which you live. Any progress would likely be significant if we first had to think about the stress on each climate mediator and the outcomes before moving forward.

5. Alternatives for Sustainable Development

Among the points of view that can establish a new level in the relationship between humanity and nature, some are characterized as perfect innovations. When they are found in our daily lives, this is a more obvious identification.

Clean innovation will provide the climate, pollute less, use all assets in more manageable items, and reuse waste. Avoid virtually zero accumulation of contaminants. Whenever contamination occurs, net profits depend on various innovations in its treatment.

The objective of the pure innovation proposal is to work on the conditions and methodology of identification by data, admission to innovation, and promotion, especially for developing countries (UNCED, 2001). In the words of Sachs (1986), "current innovations should be used to promote new products (and markets) that can improve rural biomass, park ranger services, and water supply, given the potential word associated with their creation and advice on sustainable regular assets. It is important to take into account the perspectives, beliefs, and merits of the "social actors:' such as the innovative change in their attitude and influence on their behaviour.

Meetings of people are not ready to recognize or potentially perceive the effects and results of mechanical change, and progressive progress will certainly not be fruitful to generate results, either in the expansion of the utility or economic improvement. To clean technologies to Agenda 21 (UNCED, 2001) brings propositions as:

1) if mechanical advances are not consistent with specific strategic measures to prevent harmful practices, they lead to outcomes such as impractical development methods. For example, classes get a more elegant presentation of these achievements, while the poor become significantly poorer. Actions to support the support of the planet

appear every second. Karl R. Popper (1902-1994) supports the basic realism that science is intelligent.

Presenting in science that "the proof as a logical hypothesis is a reality, that it is fragile and must be rejected': Kuhn hides the possibility that advances in science are scientific practices that are addressed by the "worldview" The moment one worldview neglects problem-solving in specific circumstances, then, at that moment, it gives way to another worldview. Improving science does not lie in the aggregation of information but in the progression of logical confusion described by "changes in the rules that order information, causing a difference in the vision of the world:' Habermas portrays modern social orders as flattened organizations, citing an instrumental logic that teaches the use of the means to achieve goals, the control of natural income, putting science and innovation to the aid of capital is one way of detailing that a financial turn of events primarily drives our innovative world. The entire theoretical premise of the prevailing philosophical worldview in culture is reflected in natural thinking in the development style and life of modern social orders.

These tests can understand the current worldview, which was based on considerations, mentalities, and actions of theft and natural decay, which also provoked social persecution, effectively giving the rule a state of inaccessibility.

a) Combination rule covers two topics: the use of prevention and maintenance assets in all structure jumps and the life cycle assessment (lifecycle assessment) of an item. LCA appeared in the world in the 70s and gained new momentum in the 90s,hoping to ensure the well-being of items and bicycles for the climate and human well-being.

b) The principle of vote-based management: bring together workers, neighbours close to the plant, buyers, and various sectors of society, based on the impact of the objects and work cycles and product creation that characterize the procedures of endurance for cleaner production.

Community right to data: this law separates concerning:

- Citizens are on the right track to know and get closer to data on the environmental state and common property;
- The right to consult and participate in making decisions that affect the climate;
- Resources and the right to be rewarded for the damage caused to the climate and human well-being.

Investing in popularity is not about developing the core values of the creative business universe; it is what professionals and buyers add to mechanical progress in a natural and socially reliable way to be more alert that players are likely to change their depreciation of the Nature in the planet. In addition, people feel that they have survived the environmental impacts caused by improvements and innovations (Peter, 2018).

The relationship between humanity and nature currently has a sustainable future projection is directed to the development of clean technologies. References to Agenda 21 (UNCED, 2001) is called "environmentally sound technologies" because protecting the environment by reducing the emission of pollutants, making use of resources in a sustainable way, their products and are willing to waste recycling.

According to Tom Sachs (1993), new products should be developed by modern technology to add value to agricultural biomass, forest, and water, linked to the use of raw materials from renewable natural resources. The rationalization of energy use, such as steam, electricity, natural gas, etc.., Replacing fossil fuels in central power production has a large effect in reducing the generation ofgaseous and particulate solids.

It is in the details for the sustainability proposal, and there must be a paradigm different from the current institutions idealize. To have a genuine quest for sustainable development, the proposals for sustainability described above reveal their intentions in need for the individuals involved in this process are aware of all the inter-relationship of each item of the process. Thus, awareness is the precursor to any attempt to seek sustainable development, which then callsfor the preparation there is a real purpose in the action of the people involved, so managing the success of the process.

5.1. C02 Issue Zero and Eco-Efficiency

In the conditions of the development of a technological civilization, the so-called crisis of consciousness is progressing, which manifests itself in a pragmatic, practical opposition of the social world to the natural. There is a depreciation of life, which becomes a commodity, an object of transformation on the part of a person to satisfy his material needs. This problem's urgency lies in need to form a new ecological consciousness that determines the worldview character of man's relationship to nature as a form of life. The greening of consciousness occurs under the influence of the reflection of immediate being - the ecological situation in residence and human activity.

Assessment of the ecological situation depends on the population's degree of awareness on the use, protection, and reproduction of natural resources, the environment, and the protection of specially protected natural areas of regional significance. It is necessary to know what is happening with the surrounding nature, what changes are taking place in it, and the tendency of their development (Peter, 2018).

This knowledge is needed to timely adjust various aspects of nature management and prevent irreversible deterioration of the state of the natural environment. The emergence of Ecology as a fact of social consciousness is a significant step forward in understanding that a person's nature is an integrated system of complex relationships, concerning which a person acts only as one of its many subsystems.

Despite the relatively young age of the formation of Ecological Consciousness - as a science, there are a large number of definitions of this concept, but they all agree on: it is a cognitive-value form of social reflection of the interaction of man (society) and nature, presented in the form of ideal or real needs and interests, having an activity, as well as an activity-oriented, universal character.

Raising environmental awareness is a complex, multifaceted process. This is, first of all, overcoming the initial passivity of a person concerning environmental problems that do not carry signs of a catastrophe, as well as the formation of the ability to assess the need for inclusion in a particular environmental situation, which is one of the factors that ensure the value of such education (Peter, 2018).

Three levels of ecological consciousness can be distinguished:

- Basic or general environmental awareness;
- Scientifically based environmental awareness;
- Professional environmental awareness. Most people have an ordinary ecological consciousness, a combination of ideas, knowledge, attitudes, and stereotypes based on everyday experience and dominating the social community they belong to. A

s a rule, egoistic elements prevail in it, taking into account, first of all, and the interests of the subject or a separate group. Ordinary consciousness tends to consider the interests of today and not think about the future (Peter, 2018).

A feature of this consciousness is the randomness of the mass of data that the consciousness operates with, the absence of any system for ordering environmental information. For most of the population, the concept of "ecological state" is always associated with any violation of the ecological situation, which is catastrophic or close to it.

Under the influence of a wide flow of information about various environmental problems, everyday environmental consciousness becomes more open to the transition from an interest in environmental news to a serious discussion of environmental problems as the initial stage of scientific, environmental consciousness.

The basis of scientifically grounded ecological consciousness is scientific knowledge; data obtained using objective research methods, and penetration into the essential relationships that characterize nature and society.

It requires proper preparation and cannot appear spontaneously. In the development of public environmental awareness, the leading role belongs to the system of continuous environmental education, including preschool, school, university, and postgraduate education, as well as the mass media (media), which creates a general atmosphere of intolerance to environmental violations and crimes.

Environmental education and enlightenment ofthe population aim to form an ecological worldview in every person and the whole society as the main condition for sustainable development (Peter, 2018).

5.2. The Environmental Awareness and Social Mobilization

Education for Sustainable Development expands the concept of environmental education, complementing it with several aspects from other fields to an integrated, interdisciplinary approach to education.

This approach to education is a continuous process throughout life, from early childhood to higher education and educational work with the population, which goes beyond formal education. At the same time, education for children is particularly important since the way of life, attitudes, and worldviews are largely formed at an early age.

Lack of environmental education work can lead to misconceptions about the inexhaustibility of the surrounding natural resources. A responsible and effective policy concerning the environment will be possible only if we accumulate reliable data on the current state of the environment, sound knowledge about the interactions of important environmental factors, develop new methods to reduce and prevent harm caused to nature by humans, and envisage the use of all economic levers (Gare, 2018).

At the present stage of environmental policy, a system of information support for environmental problems of territorial significance is needed, designed to provide information services to territories, industries, and activities using databases and services received from information centres of the first level.

Various social institutions should contribute to the greening of consciousness, and here it should be emphasized that an important component in the system of formation of environmental educational, environmental and educational activities; practical consolidation of knowledge and skills acquired in the learning process is carried out; conducting scientific research and solving practical environmental problems; vocational guidance of young people and the formation of a respectful attitude to nature. Conferences on environmental education are held in almost all regions (Gare, 2018).

As a rule, they are organized by higher educational institutions, in which teachers are professionally engaged in environmental problems. The topics of such conferences cover:

- Environmental, socio-economic;
- Environmental, and other aspects of the study and
- Development of the region, affecting the problems of public health;
- Modern methods of monitoring the natural environment, issues of environmental education of children.

The growing importance of environmental research and the growth in the number of consumers of environmental information, including the emergence of new user groups, on the one hand, and the diversification of information and documentary flows, on the other hand, created a problem and required an improvement in the system of existing industry information support.

The basic principles for developing information support systems for environmental problems were laid down by specialists.

Higher educational institutions' libraries playa great role in information support.

The ecological direction has become a noticeable phenomenon in their activities. With the greening of education and the ever-increasing need for environmental information in all sectors of the national economy and information on environmental protection, libraries are actively involved in environmental projects and grants.

The generating function of universities' libraries is that, in addition to generating external information resources, they streamline the available internal resources (in the form of author's publications of university teachers, bibliographic databases) while performing an intermediary function between the generated information flow and the consumer (Gare,2018). It is the libraries that act as resource centers and providers of environmental information, as one of the active participants in the formation of the environmental outlook of the population, having a strong experience of corporate interaction.

The library can become the leading subject of the development of ecological content and information, in essence, relations that form the ecological information space. It should be emphasized that today there is no single information system that would combine the entire range of available resources on the ecology of different regions and would allow solving the urgent problem of free access to the available environmental information of environmental structures, research institutions, universities, libraries, and other organizations. There are no guides about where and how to get environmental information, terms of provision, which publications publish it (Gare, 2018).

In USA, work has begun on the creation of a model of a unified information network (system) of environmental information, which will form a system for informing libraries, educational institutions and research organizations, schools of the territory through the targeted mailing of a block of environmental information, conducting and covering educational events on environmental education in close contact with specialists related to ecology, environmental protection, and the dissemination of environmental knowledge. For this purpose, it is planned to create a Regional Information Environmental Centre based on the PNU library for information and documentary support of environmental and environmental problems of territorial significance.

And also, an ecological portal will be created to accumulate data on the use, protection, protection, and reproduction of natural resources, environmental protection, management, and protection of specially protected natural areas of the country (Gare, 2018). A problem-oriented database (POBD)will be created for priority areas of environmental and environmental topics (conference proceedings, reports of research and development work, and research work).

This model is suitable for organizing an information support system based on a university library in any direction for scientific, educational, and educational purposes.

At the same time, the corporate interaction of scientific libraries of the Far Eastern region is a necessary condition for the development of a single information space for science and education.

Based on the presented material, it should be noted that the creation of unified information, ecological, educational, and cultural space, which would include educational institutions of all types, specially protected natural and historical and cultural territories, objects production, and service sectors, mass media and other spheres of people's life, serving the purposes of developing the ecological culture of each person and society.

5.3. Environmental Social Perception

Sociologists formulated the New Ecological Paradigm (NEP) by studying ecological movements as carriers of a new system and values. Modern society relies on attitudes that make up the Dominant Social Paradigm (DSP) based on anthropocentrism.

NEP presupposes a rejection of this principle and the recognition of man as one of many other creatures that are interdependent and included in the global ecosystem. It is based on the dominance of such ideas as the intrinsic value of nature, care for all living organisms, including people and their future generations, the desire to eliminate any types of risks and dangers that threaten humanity and nature; recognition that there are laws of the biosphere that human society should not violate (Danylova, 2018).

During this period, environmental danger and its impact on social processes became a global and clear threat to the existence of modern society, a threat not only to human health and the state of natural ecosystems but to the economic and political interests of various social groups.

As a result, the concept of risk emerged. Society is faced with the need to assess the degree of the real environmental hazard created by developing its industrial basis. Determining the likelihood of manufactured accidents and disasters has become mandatory for the management of various technological systems. At the same time, under the pressure of environmental movements in the developed countries of the West, "green" pro-Environmental Laws were adopted.

The industrial lobby needed strong arguments in the struggle to defend their interests. A quantitative risk assessment appeared, which was intended to become, on the one hand, a simple management tool, and on the other, an ideological tool in the struggle of industrial companies against the environmental movement.

Assessment became an expression of the ideology of industrialism and was intended to prove that the risk is small, and there is no environmental crisis and will not be. The protests of eco-movements and the population against dangerous objects were declared as irrational fears of non-specialists (Danylova, 2018).

In turn, the quantitative assessment of the risk caused a sharply negative reaction from the ecological community and distrust of the population. Anthropologists and sociologists have proven that public rejection of this approach and growing concern about environmental and technological risks are not irrational but higher rationality. Society must decide what it considers most dangerous. The most important step towards risk assessment was taken by Charles Perrow, who introduced the concept of a systemic accident. He made a detailed analysis of several accidents and concluded that complex technologies are the culprit of the disasters.

The likelihood of a failure occurring in the interaction between their elements cannot be calculated by analyzing the probabilities of failure in each of them. Further development of risk research led to the emergence of the concept of risk society by W. Beck in 1984. Beck brought the concept of a systemic incident outside the narrow framework of the functioning of technological systems, defining modern society as a society of risk, which is universal, unpredictable, and valuable. Society and its institutions are forced to assess their actions from the standpoint of risk acceptability constantly. It is this process that Beck and his followers define as reflexive modernization.

5.4. Politics and Environment

Co-evolution as a new paradigm for developing the "nature-society-man" system Man has two worlds. One created it, and man created the other world according to his understanding. It is the natural world and the world of artificial nature.

They are linked to each other through man and his activity, which assumes mutual evolution. There is a relationship and interaction, causation. It is the possibility of co-evolution of the natural world and the human world.

The emergence of man in the course of the evolution of nature meant that earlier man was in the care of Mother Nature, and now, as her son, he must take responsibility for the fate of nature. The global problems of our time, the reality of the ecological crisis urgently demand to change the European paradigm of "human exclusivity:' to revise the principle of anthropocentrism in favour of a new natural philosophy- the philosophy of co evolution.

The co-evolutionary strategy makes it possible to comprehensively comprehend the anthropogenic impact on nature, predict the situation, and develop recommendations for an optimal attitude to nature. The idea of co evolution insistently requires considering as an object of philosophical analysis, not nature or man, but the relation of "nature-society-man:' the relationship between the biosphere and the no sphere; interconnection and interaction of nature, culture, and civilization.

The idea of co-evolution forms a special ecological consciousness of a person standing in front of the face of nature in the range from reverence and questioning to "after me - even though the grass does not grow:' It forms a person's critical view of the world and himself, teaches him to make decisions independently, focusing not on an abstract but a real concrete situation.

The idea of co evolution casts doubt on the technocratic paradigm of thinking, which considers the ecological crisis as something external to man. Since it is generated by technical progress, then, therefore, it is necessary to edit this progress, introduce new technologies, and rely on waste-free production.

So far, practice shows that these are half measures; if the issue of changing human qualities is not resolved, a person's worldview does not change. Today there are three needs for the birth of a new philosophy of nature as a philosophy of co-evolution: general cultural, scientific, and philosophical.

Man needs a philosophy of nature as a substantiation of the integrity of the world and man, the restoration of organic ties with nature, in the formation of a measure of responsibility to nature, in the establishment of a dialogue with the natural world. The time of fixation on anthropocentrism or biocentrism has passed; an era has come when it is necessary to consider the co-evolution of nature and society, their self-organizing principle, the entelechy of the 21st century as an object of philosophical analysis.

If self-organization deals with the structure, the state of a particular system, then co-evolution - with the relations between self-organizing systems, with the correlation of their evolutionary changes, which are coupled with each other, mutually adapted. The conjugation of systems and their mutual adaptability presuppose the possibility of cooperation based on mutual assistance and solidarity principles. Co-evolution is destroying the old image of war of all against all. It proposes not expansion but a dialogue based on recognizing the mutual value of nature and man.

Since co-evolution presupposes special corporatism, solidarity between man and nature, this unity is already beyond the bounds of natural science. It became the object of the philosophy of nature (new natural philosophy). The term "co-evolution" appeared in the early 70s when the negative consequences of the scientific and technological revolution began to affect.

It meant the mutual adaptation of species, which can be different from mutually beneficial to the relationship between master and slave, predator and prey. When it comes to co-evolution in the "nature-society-man" system, then only the type of mutual adaptation based on a mutual benefit is assumed, considering the specific level of development of both nature and man.

The situation of mutually beneficial adaptation is complicated because nature develops according to its laws and society - according to its own. Unlike nature, human evolution is conditioned by both biological and socio-cultural factors. In nature, elements rule the ball, in society - consciousness.

Knowledge of these features and considering the specifics of the evolutionary factors of both nature and man makes it possible to fix the relative stability of biological and geographical factors and the relative variability of the socio-cultural factor.

The milestones of co-evolution in the "nature-society-man" system is:

- Transition from parasitism and consumerism to respectful attitude and symbiosis;
- The implementation by society and man of the principle of harmony - such a connection of world perception, world outlook, which ensures a person's awareness of himself as a particle of nature, genetically related to it, and therefore inseparable from it;
- Implementation of the principle of personal responsibility of each person for life on Earth;
- Awareness not only of its dependence on nature but also of nature's dependence on society and each person. These are not just abstract moral precepts or rules but of paramount importance for solving man's survival and nature itself.

In people's minds, an idea should be formed that could unite all earthlings into one whole. Only the idea of harmony can be such an idea that the entire history of humankind shreds of evidence, and social evolution must be in harmony with biological evolution.

The need to resolve global problems dictates the rejection of narrow class, group, national, regional interests and the transition to universal human interests.

The human race is united by a single destiny unity with nature. The technological type of thinking should give way to the no sphere type of thinking, focused on restoring the broken cycle of the turnover of substances and energy of the biosphere, ensuring biological stability and no sphere balance (Suzdaleva, 2020).

Experts believe that the environment can shape or neutralize each person's behaviour in the event of inadequately motivated reinforcement. Behavioural psychology can provide examples of positive behavioural motivation and teach everyone to respond appropriately to open contacts. Educational programs, positive experience, competence, and social support systems are specific help focused on correcting unmotivated actions. Having the ability to see mistakes, you can easily correct them by applying a scientific approach to solving the problem.

Due to environmental pollution, there is a decrease in soil fertility, degradation, and desertification of lands, death of flora and fauna, deterioration of the quality of atmospheric air, surface, and ground waters. Taken together, this leads to the disappearance of entire ecosystems and biological species from the face of the Earth, deterioration of public health, and a decrease in the life expectancy of people.

About 85% of all diseases of a modern person are associated with unfavourable environmental conditions arising from his fault. Many diseases have become more difficult to heal than before.

Therefore, the "Human health and the environment" problem is now very acute (Suzdaleva, 2020). Environmental factors such as changes in atmospheric pressure, air humidity, the electromagnetic field of the planet, precipitation in the form of rain or snow, movement of atmospheric fronts, cyclones, gusts of wind - lead to a change in well-being.

They can cause headaches, exacerbation of joint diseases, and changes in blood pressure. But weather changes affect different people in different ways. If a person is healthy, his body will quickly become attuned to new climatic conditions, and unpleasant sensations will bypass him.

A sick or weakened human body has an impaired ability to quickly tune in to weather changes, so it suffers from general malaise and pain (Suzdaleva,2020). The manufactured activity of people leads to an increase in the release of industrial waste into the environment. Chemical compounds from waste enter the soil, air, and water, and then, through the use of contaminated food and water, inhalation of air saturated with harmful elements enters the body. As a result, all human organs, including the brain, contain several milligrams of poisons that poison life. Exposure to toxic substances can cause nausea, coughing, and dizziness. If they regularly get inside, then chronic poisoning may develop. Its signs are rapid fatigue, constant fatigue, insomnia or drowsiness, apathy, frequent mood swings, impaired attention, psychomotor reactions. Government and organizational measure are need every country worldwide. Policies have a direct relation with the Environmental problem solving.

References

AITALIEVA, N.R., 2018. Bureaucracy and Public Trust. Global Encyclopedia ofPublic Administration, Public Policy, and Governance. Springer. Doi, 10, pp.978-3. AID, M.M., 2013. Measurement and signature intelligence. In Routledge Companion to Intelligence Studies (pp. 132-140). Routledge.

ARORA, N.K., Fatima, T., Mishra, I., Verma, M., Mishra, J. and Mishra, v., 2018. Environmental sustainability: challenges and viable solutions. Environmental Sustainability, 1(4), pp.309-340. BURDETT, K., 2012. Towards a theory of the labor market with a public sector. Labour economics, 19(1), pp.68-75.

BLOMKAMP, E.,2018. The promise ofco-design for public policy.Australian Journal ofPublic Administration, 77(4), pp.729-743.

CHAPMAN, C.R.A., 2019. Ethics in public service. Edinburgh University Press. CAPARINI, M. and Born, H., 2016. Controlling and overseeing intelligence services in democratic states. In Democratic Control of Intelligence Services (pp. 25-46). Routledge.

CRIEKEMANS, D., 2011, March. The geopolitics of renewable energy: different or similar to the geopolitics of conventional energy. In ISA Annual Convention (pp. 16-19).

DENHARDT, R.B., Denhardt,J.V. and Blanc,T.A., 2013.Public administration: An action orientation. Cengage Learning. DUTT, P. and Mitra, D., 2010. Impacts ofideology, inequality, lobbying, and public finance. The political economy of agricultural price distortions, pp.278-303.

DANYLOVA, T. and Salata, G., 2018. The ecological imperative and human nature: A new perspective on ecological education. Interdisciplinary studies of complex system, (12), pp.17-24.

ENWEREUZOR, I.K.,Adeyemi, B.A.and Onyishi, I.E.,2020.Trust in leader as a pathway between ethical leadership and safety compliance. Leadership in Health Services. 204 EHRLICH,

P.R. and Ehrlich, A.H., 2013. Can a collapse ofglobal civilization be avoided? Proceedings of the Royal Society B: Biological Sciences, 280(1754), p.20122845. FOX, R.M. and DeMarco, J.P., 2020. The challenge of applied ethics. In New directions in ethics (pp. 1-18). Routledge.

FREDERICKSON, H.G. and Rohr, J.A., 2015. Ethics and public administration. Routledge. FARMER, D.J., 2015. Public administration in perspective: Theory and practice through multiple lenses. Routledge.

GELDERMAN, C.J., Semeijn, J. and Vluggen, R., 2017. Development of sustainability in public sector procurement. Public Money& Management, 37(6), pp.435-442.

GUERAS, D. and Garofalo, c., 2010. Practical ethics in public administration. Berrett-Koehler Publishers. GILL, P., 2012.Policing politics: security intelligence and the liberal democratic state. Routledge.

GORTA, A., 2016. Corruption risk areas and corruption resistance. In Measuring corruption (pp. 219-236). Routledge.

GRAY, C.S., 2014. Strategy and defence planning: meeting the challenge of uncertainty. Oxford University Press, USA. GODWIN, K., Ainsworth, S.H. and Godwin, E., 2012. Lobbying and policymaking: The public pursuit of private interests. Cq Press.

GRATTAN, R., Parry, G. and O'Regan, N., 2011. The strategic defence review 1998: Politics, power and influence in government decisions.

GIBLER, D.M., 2010. Outside-in: The effects of external threat on state centralization. Journal ofConflict Resolution, 54(4), pp.519-542 GARE, A., 2018. Ethics, philosophy and the environment. Cosmos and History: The Journal ofNatural and Social Philosophy, 14(3), pp.219-240.

HANSON, J.K., 2015. Democracy and state capacity: complements or substitutes? Studies in comparative international development, 50(3), pp.304-330.

KELLY, E.M., Greeny, K., Rosenberg, N. and Schwartz, I., 2021. When rules are not enough: Developing principles to guide ethical conduct. Behaviour 205 Analysis in Practice, 14(2), pp.491-498.

KRAHMANN, E., 2010. States, citizens and the privatisation of security. Cambridge University Press.

KACZOROWSKA-IRELAND, A., 2015. Public international law. Routledge.

LAWTON, A. and Macaulay, M., 2015. Ethics management and ethical management. In Ethics and integrity in public administration: Concepts and cases (pp. 119-132). Routledge.

LIKHOTAL, A., 2014. Environmental Acceptability as the Driver of New Civilization. Cadmus, 2(2), p.24.

MCCANN, J.and Sweet, M., 2014. The perceptions of ethical and sustainable leadership. Journal ofBusiness Ethics, 121(3), pp.373-383.

MANTALUTA, A., 2019. Lobbying: the relationship between state, market and the public sector. In Symposium Scientific International al Tinerilor Cercetatori (pp. 71-76).

MOKROSINSKA, D., 2020. Why states have no right to privacy, but may be entitled to secrecy: a non-consequentialist defense of state secrecy. Critical Review ofInternational Social and Political Philosophy, 23(4), pp.415-444.

MCELREATH, D.H., Doss, D.A., Russo, B.,Etter, G., Van Slyke,J., Skinner, J., Corey, M., Jensen, C.J.,Wigginton, M. and Nations, R.,2021. Introduction to homeland security. CRC Press.

NEVONDWE, 1., Odeku, K.O.and Raligilia,K.,2014. Ethics in the state-owned companies in the public sector: a thin line between corporate governance and ethical leadership. Mediterranean Journal of Social Sciences, 5(15), pp.661-661.

PLANT, J.E, 2018. Responsibility in public administration ethics. Public Integrity, 20(supl), pp.S33-S45.

PLAN, B.C., Model, T.1. and Blog, H.D.I., 2018. Ethical management.

PAPHITI, A., 2011. 'Intervention in the Internal Affairs of States. E-International Relations Publishing.

PETER, S.C., 2018. Reduction of C02 to chemicals and fuels: a solution to global warming and energy crisis. ACSEnergy Letters, 3(7), pp.1557-1561.

PALTSEV, S.,2016. The complicated geopolitics ofrenewable energy. Bulletin 206 ofthe Atomic Scientists, 72(6), pp.390-395.

RAND NATIONAL DEFENSE RESEARCH INST SANTAMONICA CA. YANG, P., 2020. Toward a framework for (re) thinking the ethics and politics of international student mobility. Journal of Studies in International Education, 24(5), pp.518-534.

REUTER, C. ed., 2019. Information Technology for Peace and Security: IT Applications and Infrastructures in Conflicts, Crises, War, and Peace. Springer.

RISTOVSKI, L., 2017. Morality and ethics in politics in the contemporary societies. Journal ofLiberty and International Affairs, 2(03), pp.83-93.

ROHR, J.A. and Storing, H.J., 2017. Ethics for bureaucrats: An essay on law and values. Routledge.

ROMERO, M.C., 2020. Teaching ethics for professional practice. In The Handbook of Professional, Ethical and Research Practice for Psychologists, Counsellors, Psychotherapists and Psychiatrists (pp. 217-231). Routledge.

SANO, J., 2015. The changing shape of HUMINT. Intelligencer Journal, 21(3), pp.77-80.

SONGKLIN, P., 2017.Ethics in Public Administration: Theoretical Foundation. In Proceedings ofthe International

Conference on Ethics in Governance (ICONEG 2016). Paris, France: Atlantis Press. https:lldoi. org/lO.299l! iconeg-16.2017 (Vol. 87).

STEHR, N., & Machin, A. (2020). Society and climate: Transformations and challenges.

SHALVI, S., Dana, J., Handgraaf, M.J. and De Dreu, C.K., 2011. Justified ethicality: Observing desired counterfactuals modifies ethical perceptions and behavior. Organizational Behavior and Human Decision Processes, 115(2), pp.181-190.

SCHAURER, F. and Storger,J.,2013. The evolution ofopen source intelligence (OSINT). Comput Hum Behav, 19, pp.53-56. URSUL, A. and Ursul, T., 2018. Environmental education for sustainable development. Future Human Image, 9(1), p.116.

SUMRA, K., 2019. Public Service Ethics in Public Administration: An Empirical Investigation. International Journal of Law and Political Sciences, 13(10), pp.1338-1349.

TANNY, ET. and Al-Hossienie, C.A., 2019. Trust in Government: Factors Affecting Public Trust and Distrust. [ahangimagar Journal of Administrative Studies, Department ofPublic Administration, 12, p.52.

TUAN, L.T., 2012. Corporate social responsibility, ethics, and corporate governance. Social Responsibility Journal.

TSIAMIS, A., Gatsis, K. and Pappas, G.J., 2018, December. An information matrix approach for state secrecy.In 2018 IEEE Conference on Decision and Control (CDC) (pp. 2062-2067). IEEE. SHAKEEL, E, Kruyen, P.M. and Van Thiel, S., 2019. Ethical leadership as process: A conceptual proposition. Public Integrity, 21(6), pp.613-624. SHAFRITZ, J., Russell, E.W:, Borick,C. and Hyde, A., 2016.Introducing public 207 administration. Routledge. SUZDALEVA, A., 2020. Ecological globalistics and the paradigm of world civilization development. In E3SWeb ofConferences (Vol. 217, p. 11003). EDP Sciences.

VARELA, M.D.M.C., 2019. The ethical state? In Reimagining the State (pp. 97-113). Routledge.

VISHWAKARMA, V. and Kirubaharan, A.K., 2021. Ethical Issues and Environmental Safety. Polymetallic Coatings to Control Biofouling in Pipelines: Challenges and Potential, p.l07. WEGGE, N., 2017. Intelligence Oversight and the Security of the State. International Journal of Intelligence and CounterIntelligence, 30(4), pp.687-700.

WEINBAUM, C., Berner, S. and McClintock, B., 2017. SIGINT for anyone: The growing availability of signals intelligence in the public domain.

ZAK, M., 2019. Democracy, lobbying and economics. Review ofEconomic Perspectives, 19(3), pp.193-21O

About the Author

Artur Victoria is a Researcher at OBSERVARE – Observatory of Foreign Relations of the Autonomous University of Lisbon (UAL) and lecturer in non-governmental organizations,

Graduated in Law in the University of Lisbon. Degree in Defense Course and holds certificates such as: Trainer of Trainers (BAR Association, update course at the National Defense Institute, Diploma on Corruption Control (Open Society Hungary) .He was the founder of the Colegio Luso Internacional - CLIP in Portugal, President of the European representative of the Portuguese Culture Federation, Founder and President of the Brazilian – Portuguese Law Institute - , Representative in Europe of the Association of Graduates of the Escola de Diplomados Superior de Guerra - Brazil.

He practiced law for 21 years - he was an elected member of the District Council of the Portuguese Bar Association of Lawyers and a trainee advisor at the BAR Association.

Author of five law books, he writes articles on ethics and security for academic websites.

Official commendations:

- 2014 Brazil - Friend of the Navy Medal (Brazilian Navy)

2015 - Portugal- Medal of Merit of the Portuguese Army D.Afonso Henriques - silver grade

2015 - Brazil- Order of Merit Aeronautico (Knight) of the Brazilian Air Force

2019 Brazil - Medalha Tamandare (Brazilian Navy)

2020- Brazil - Order of Naval Merit – Knight (Brazilian Navy)

2021 - Portugal - Medal of the Cross of St. George 1st degree

2020 - Brazil -Ordem do Merito promoted to Officer (Brazilian Air Force)

2021 Brazil - Order of Naval Merit – (Brazilian Navy)

2023 Brazil-Order de Rio Branco – given by the President of Republic of Brazil

Read more at https://observare.autonoma.pt/investigador/artur-victoria/.

www.ingramcontent.com/pod-product-compliance
Lightning Source LLC
LaVergne TN
LVHW091303150826
845673LV00006B/1525

* 9 7 9 8 2 3 0 1 6 4 0 9 8 *